This Book Belongs to:

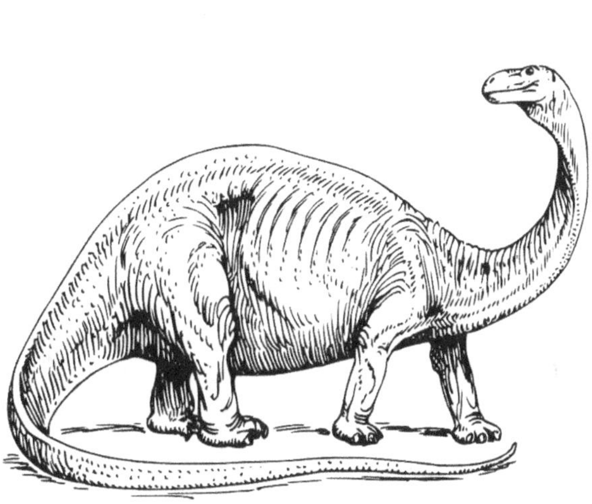

C.P.©
Carreira publications

Test Color Page

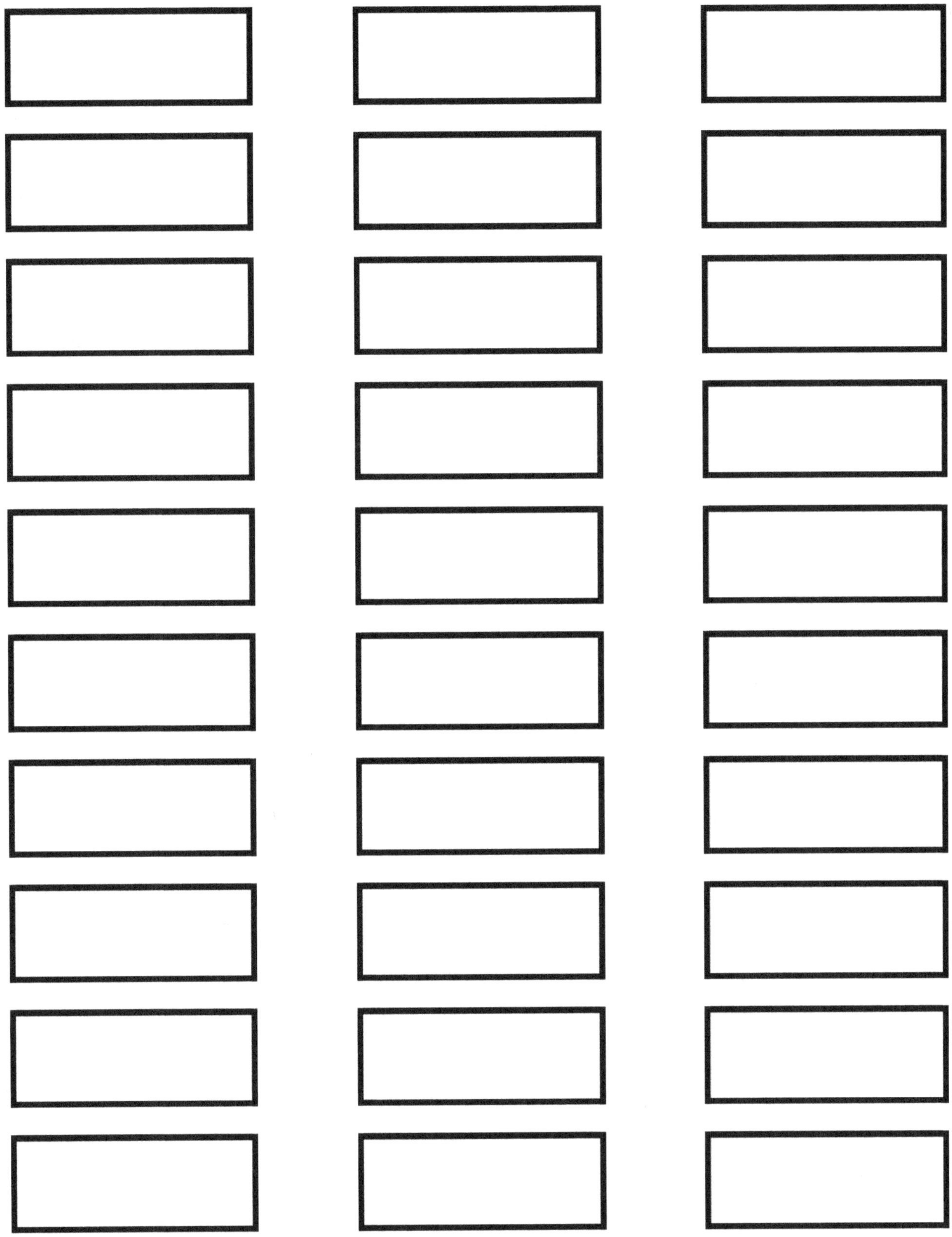

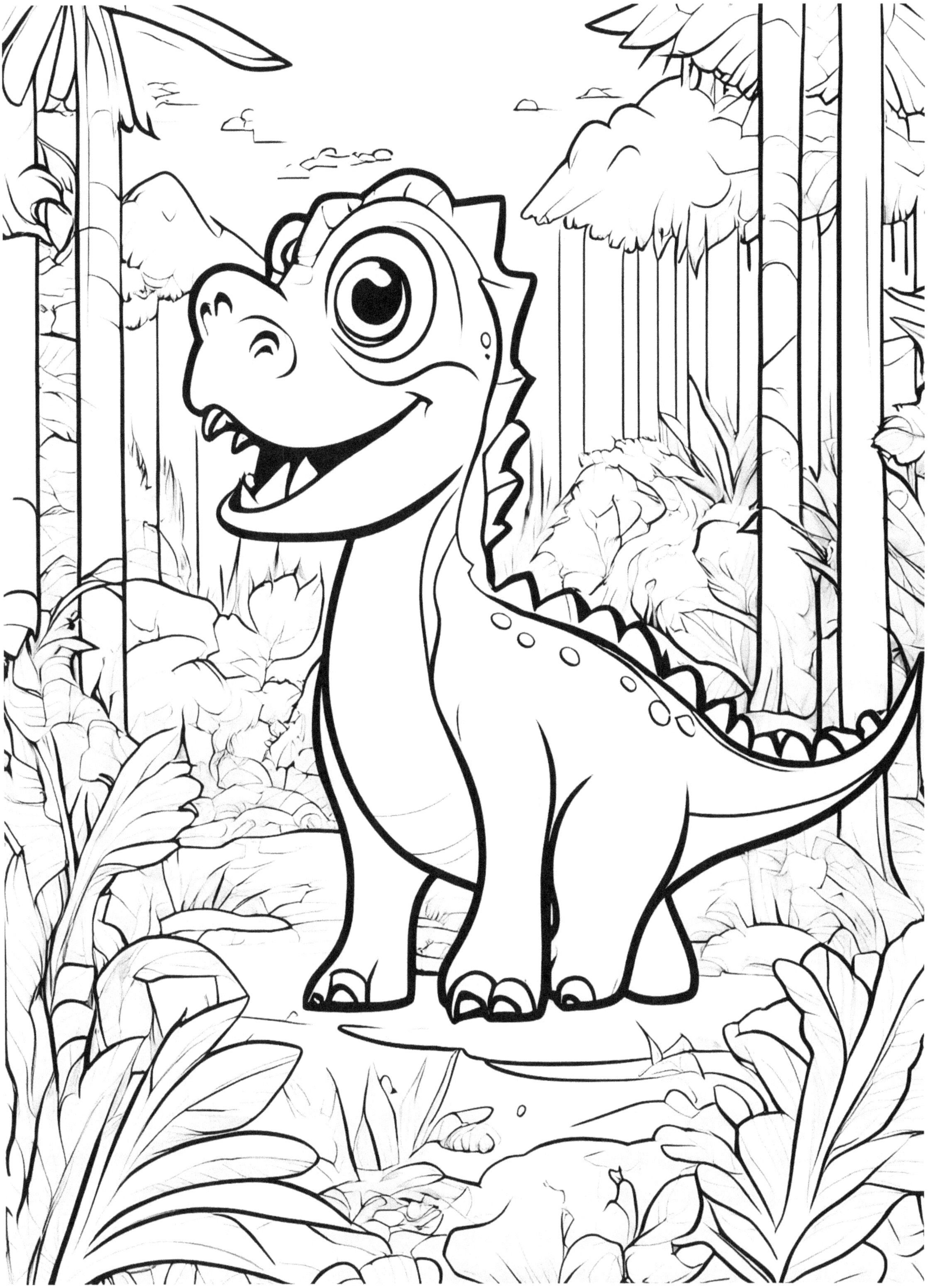

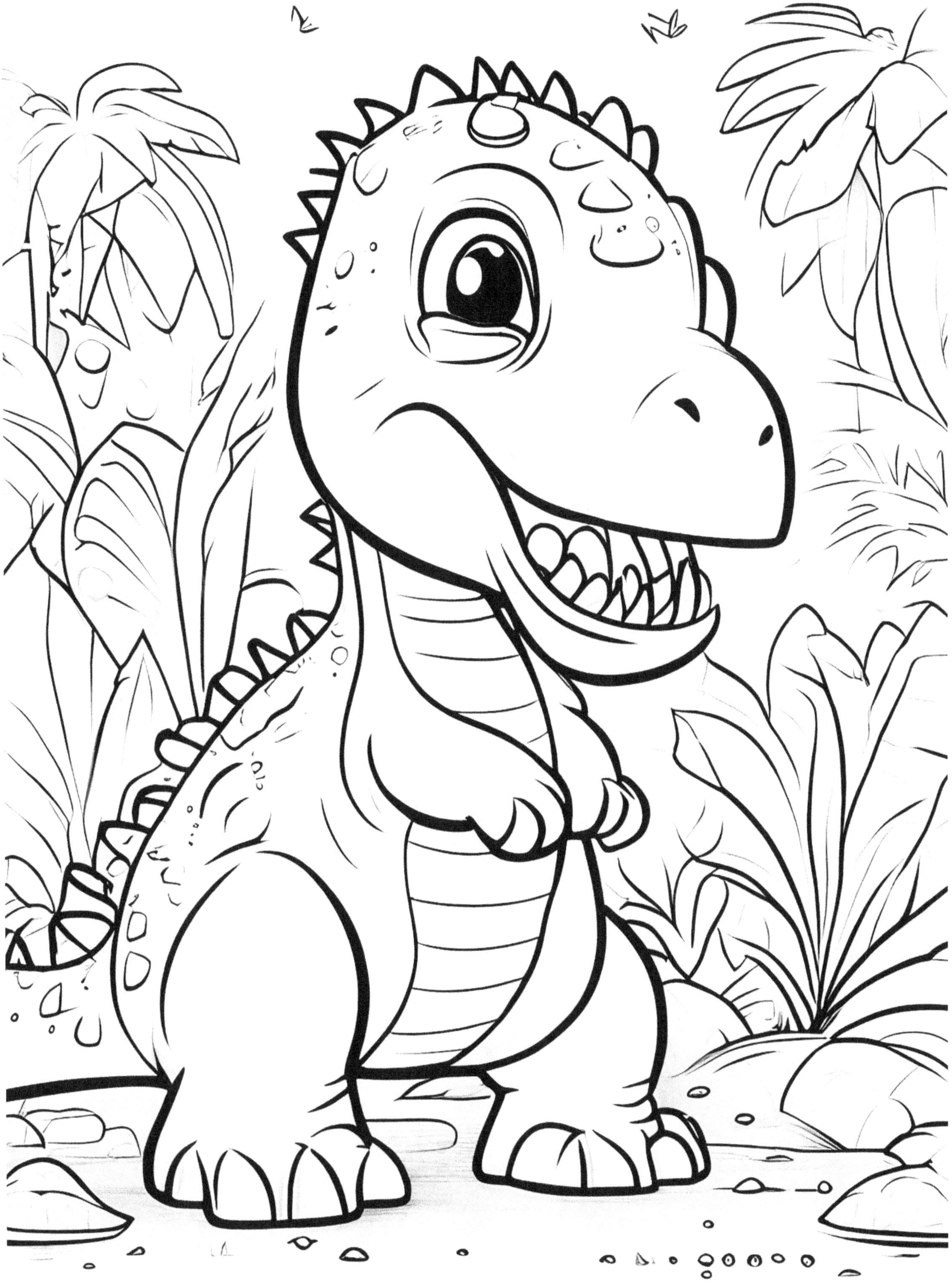

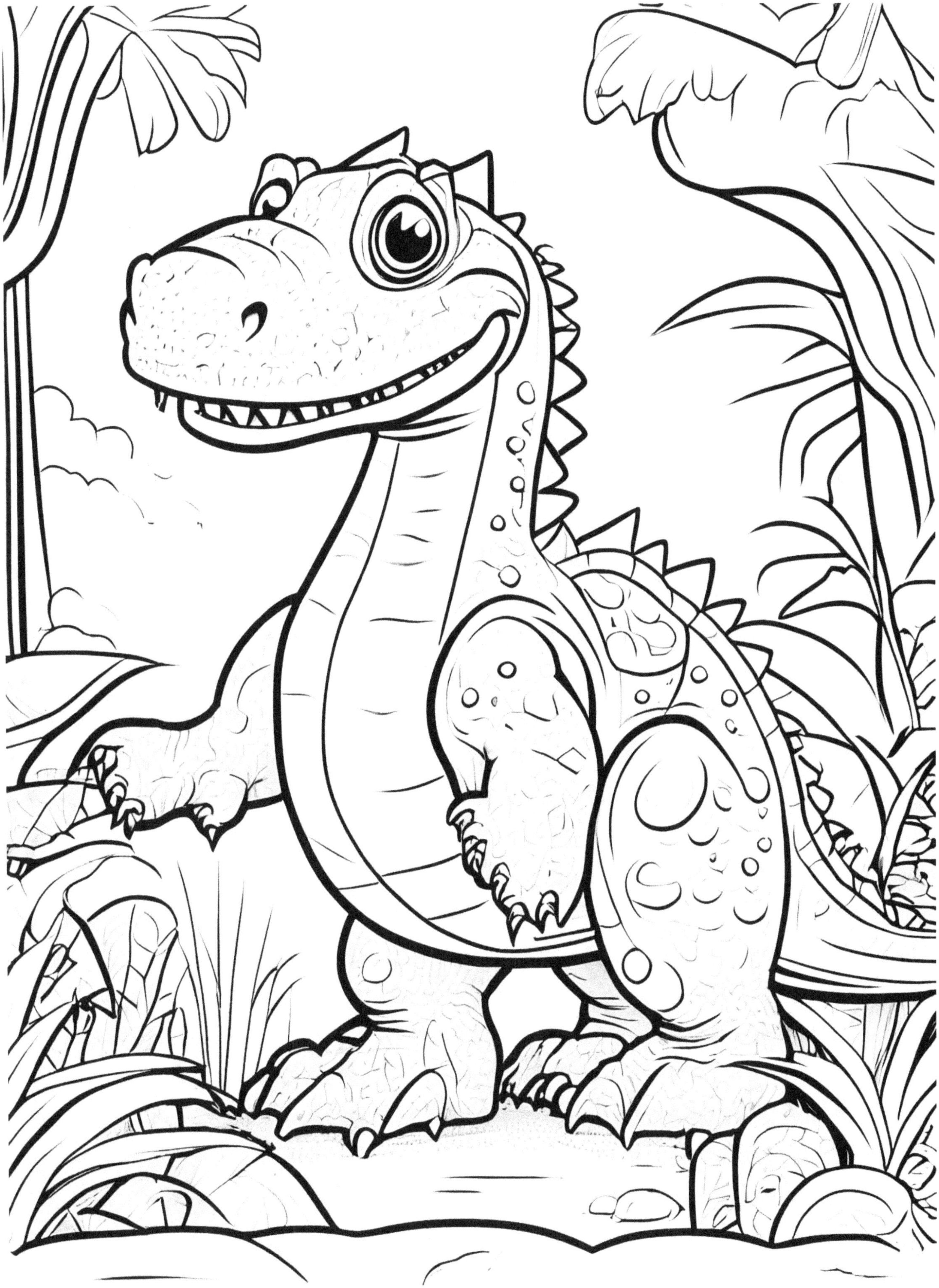

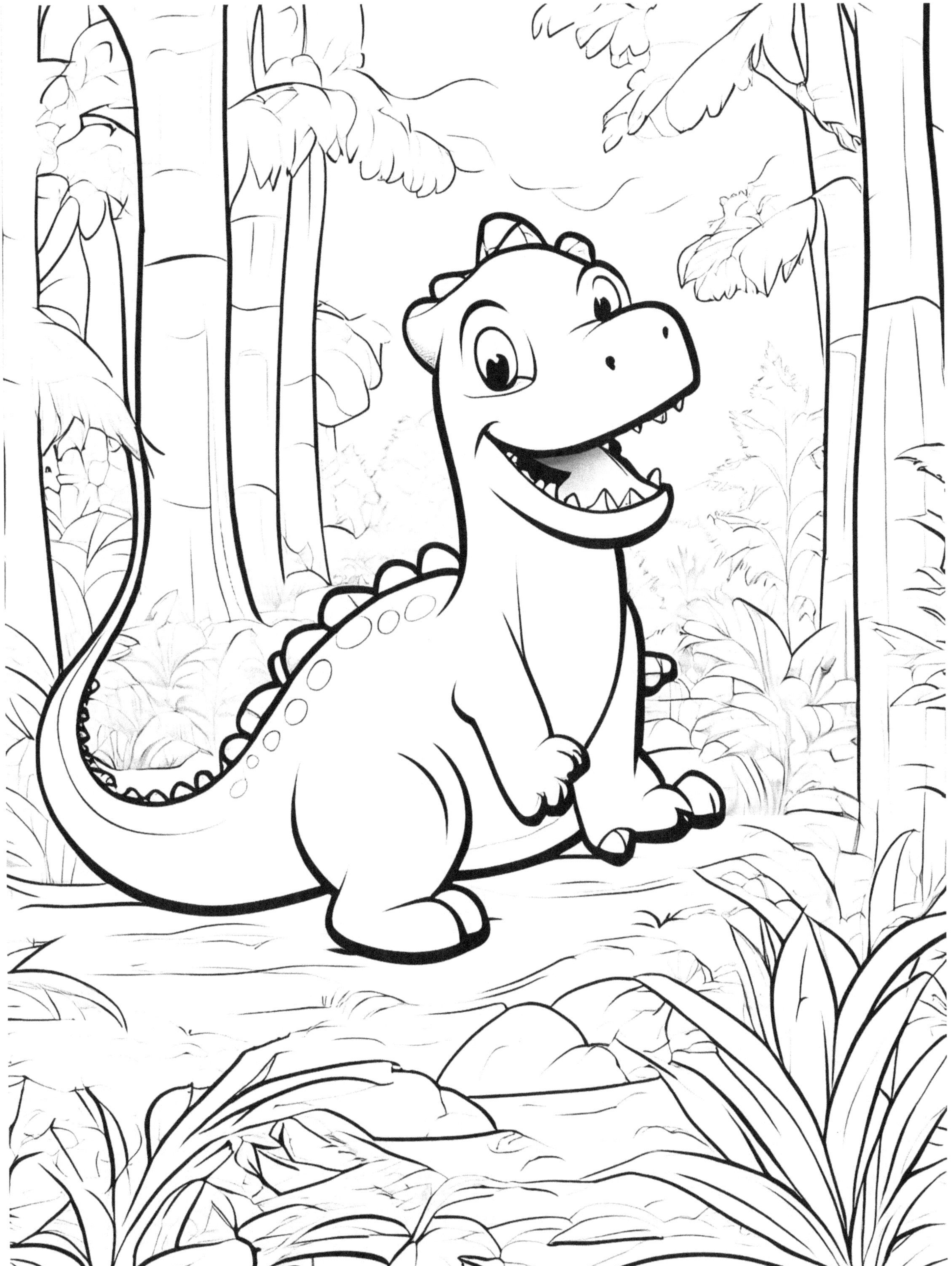

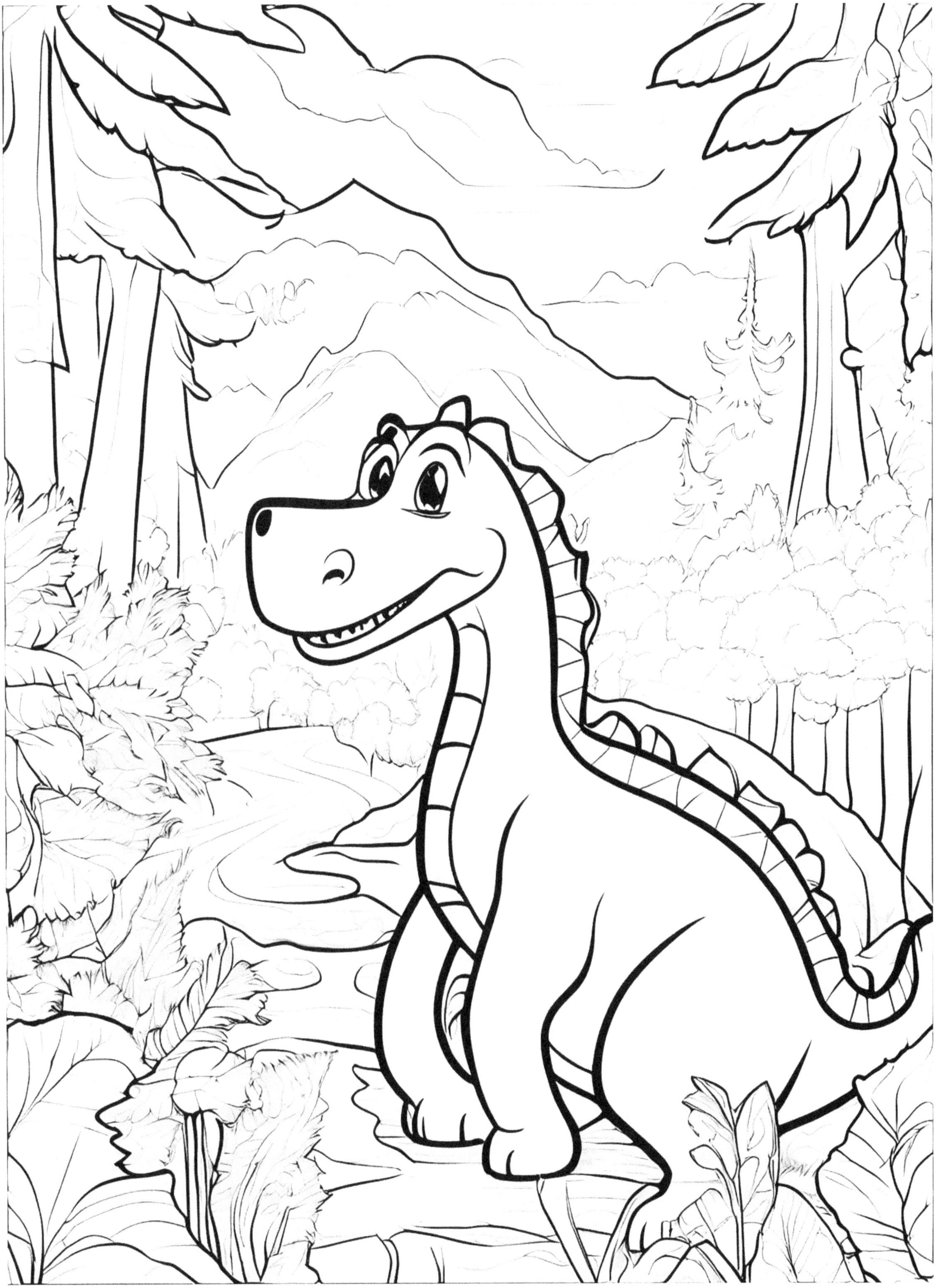

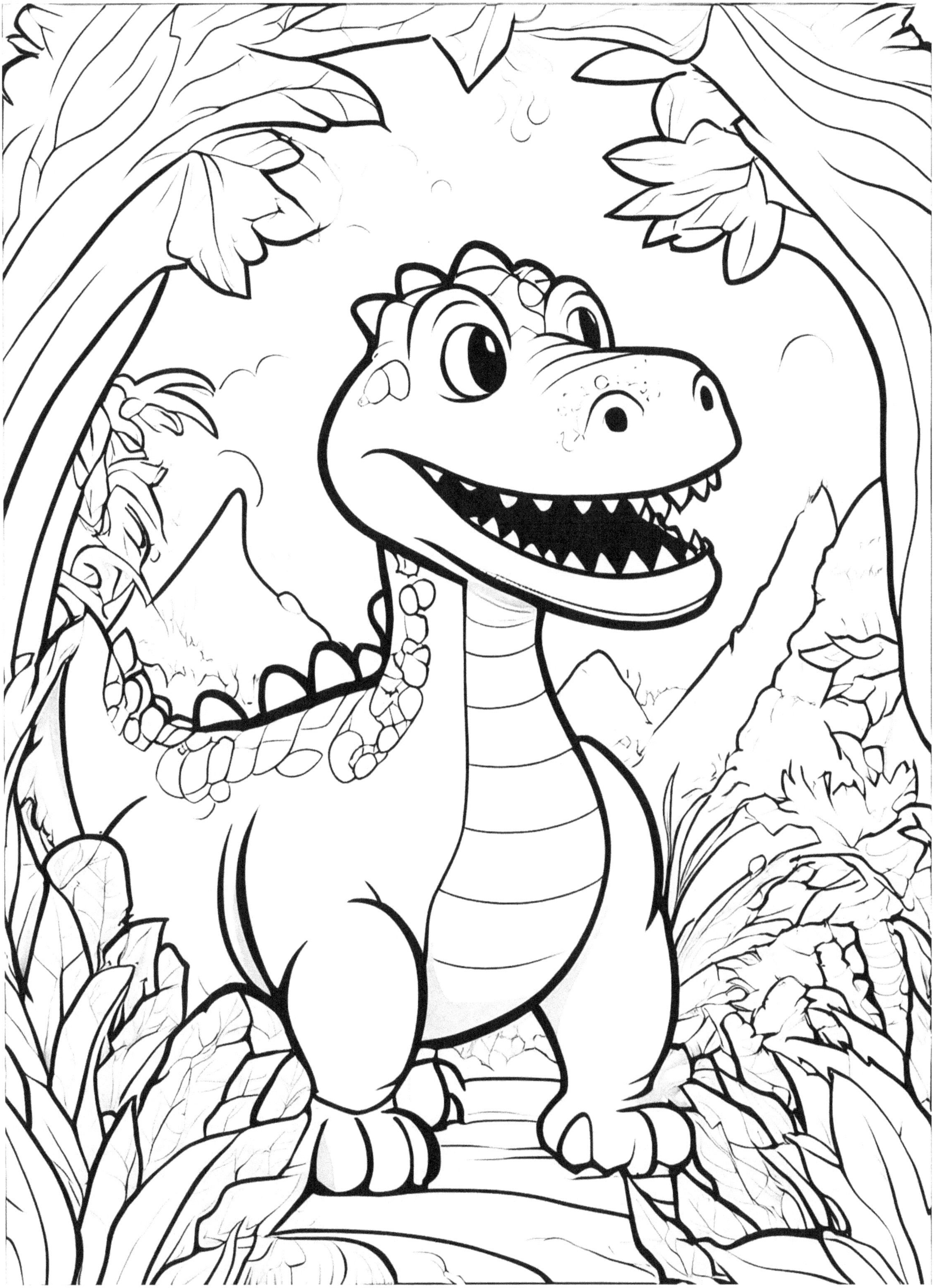

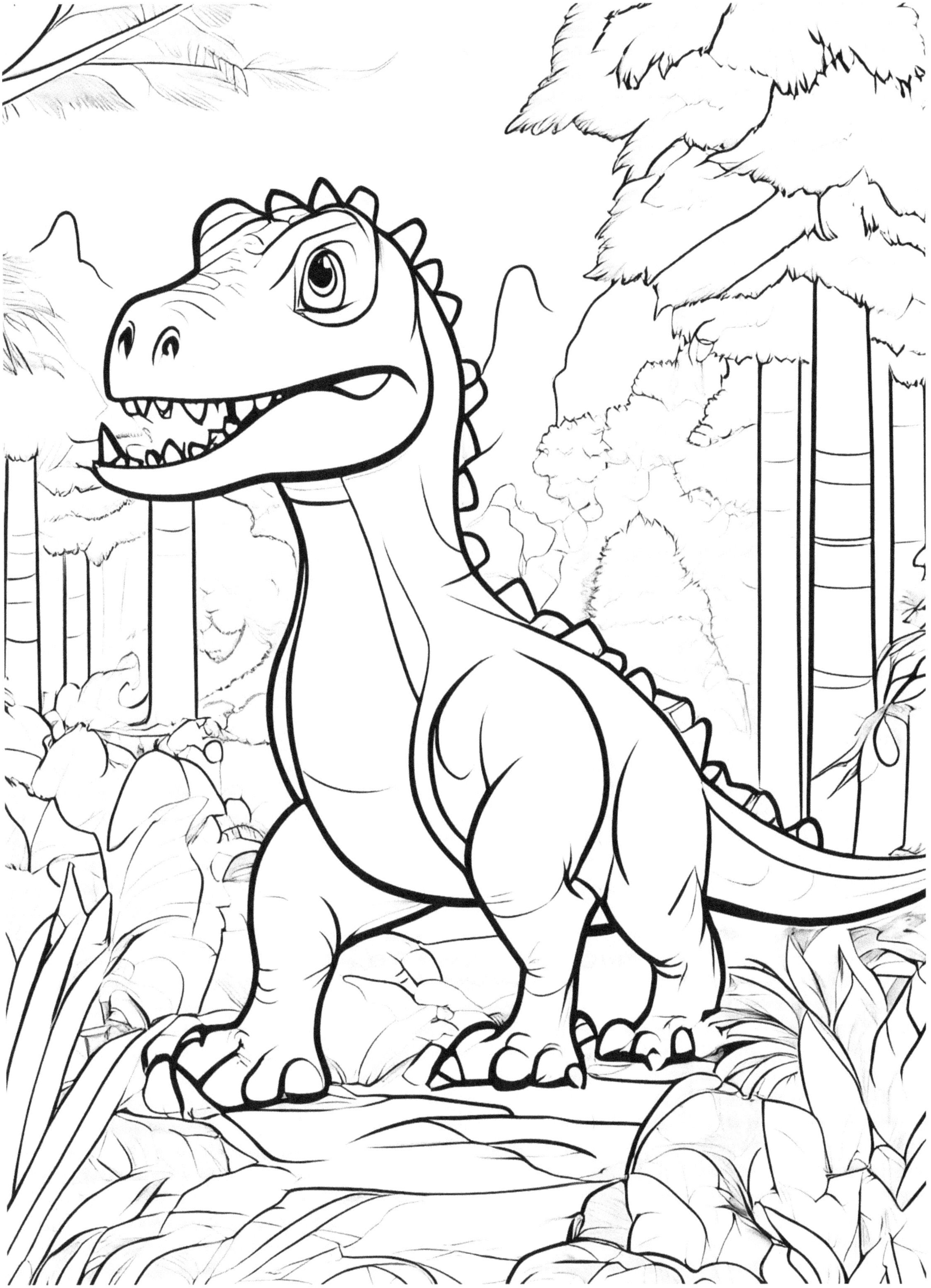

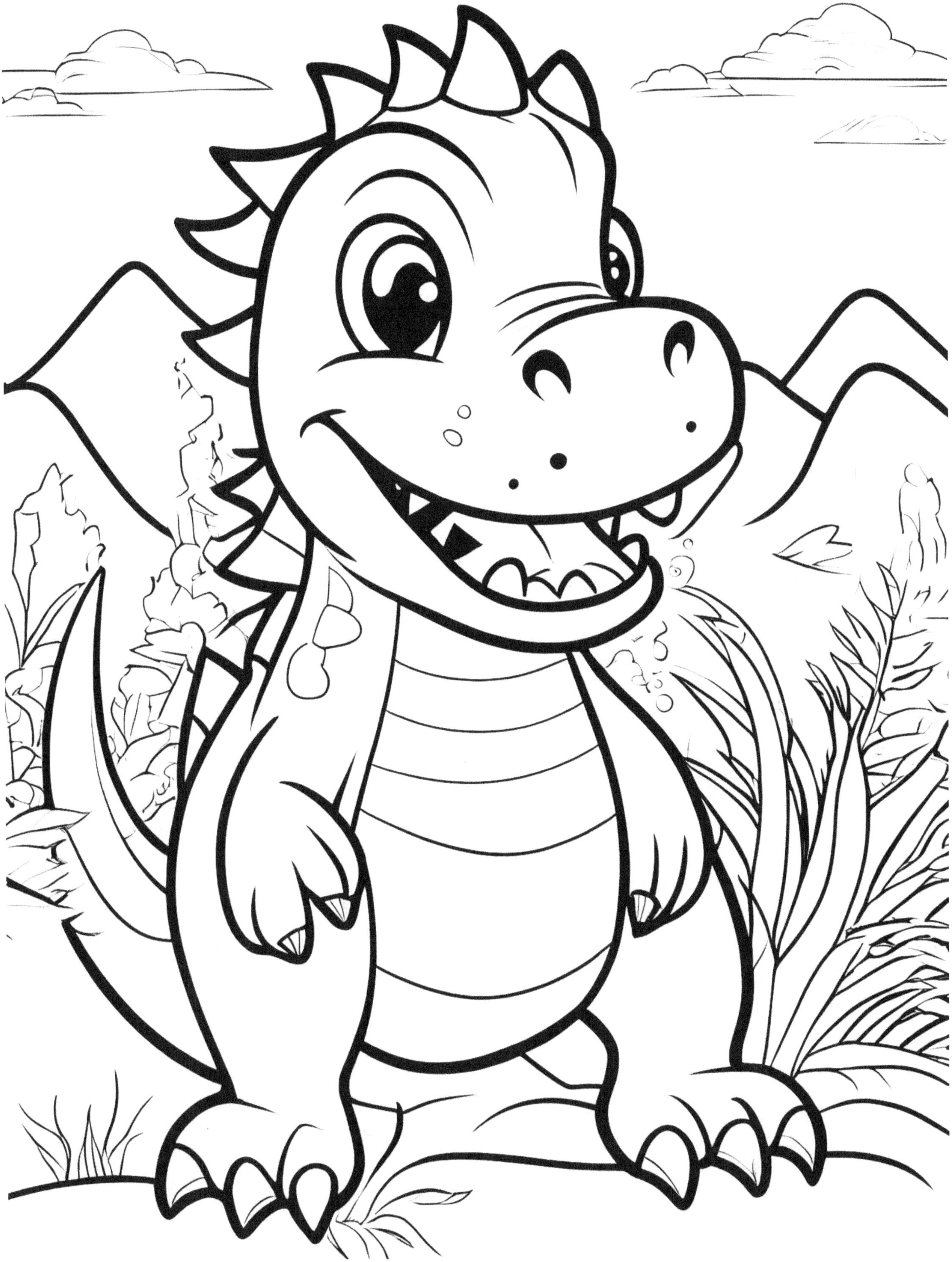

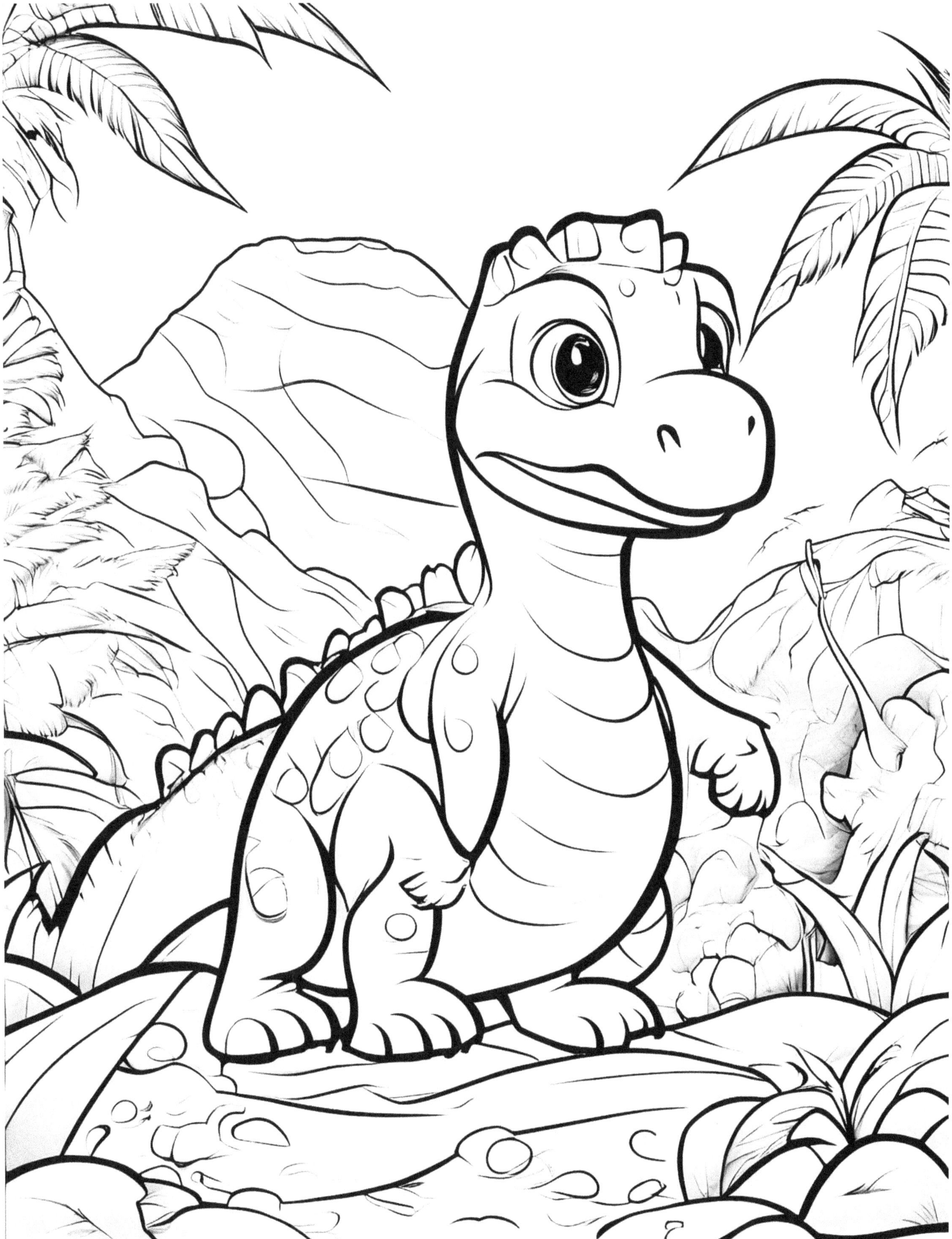

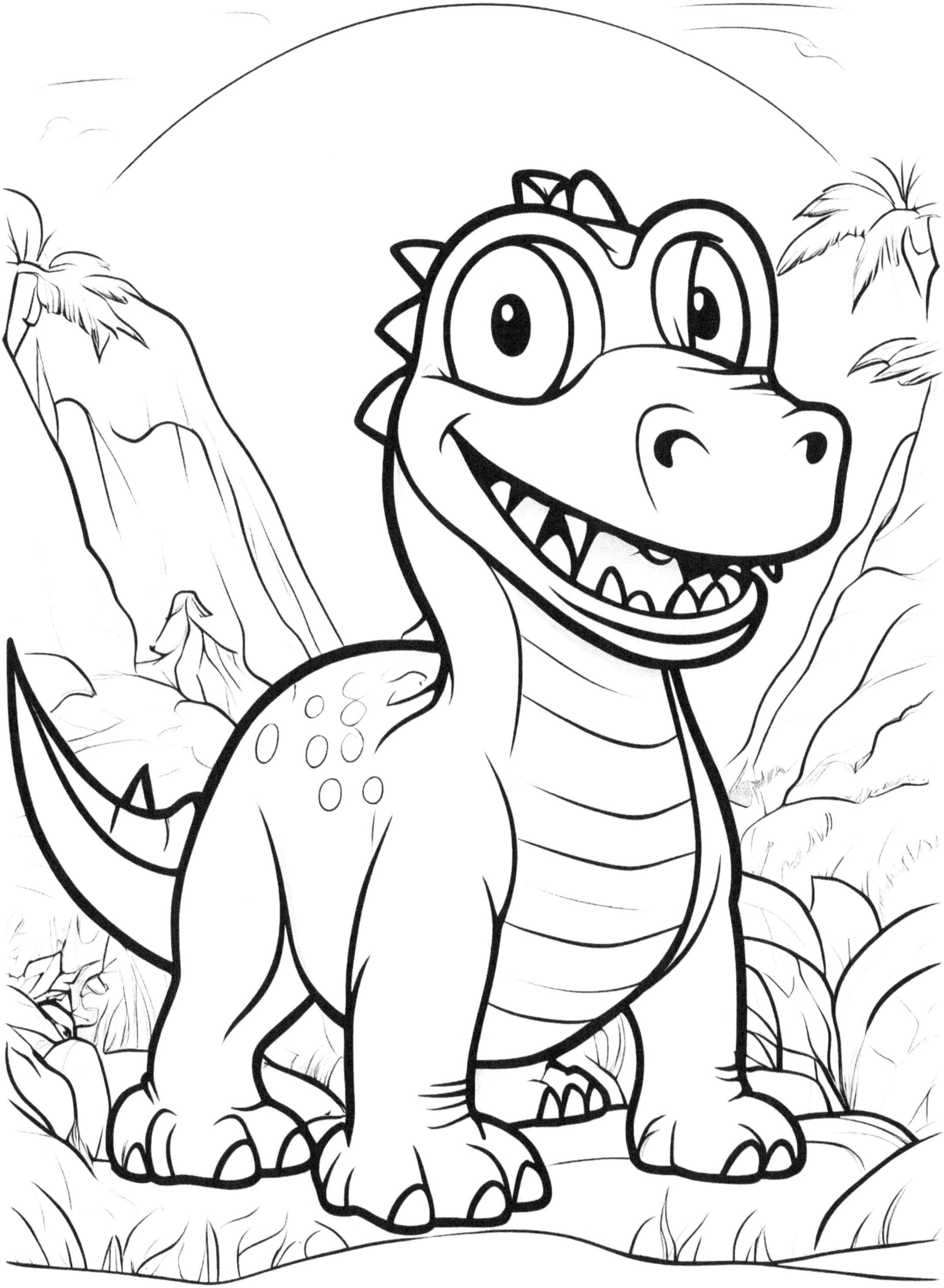

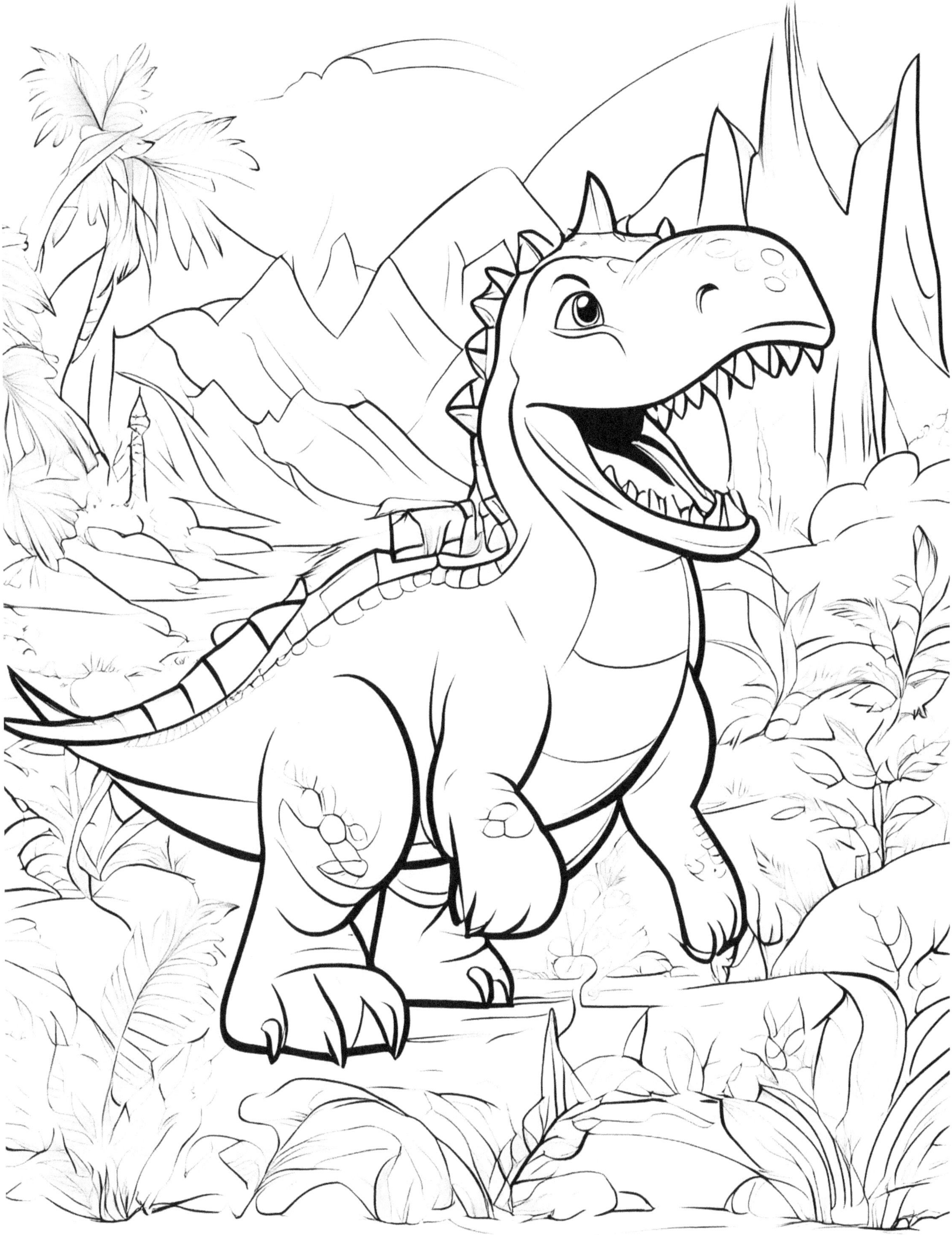

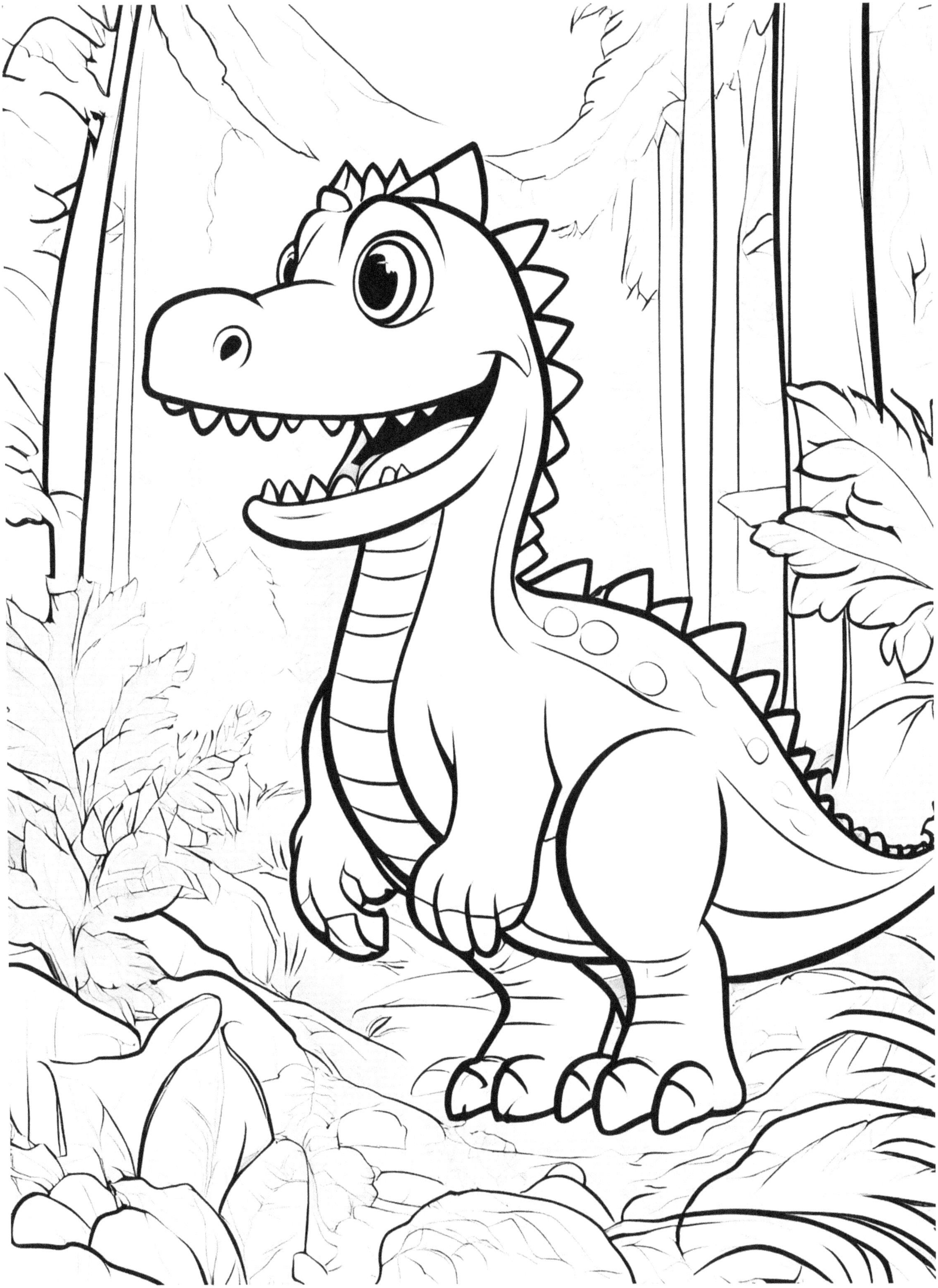

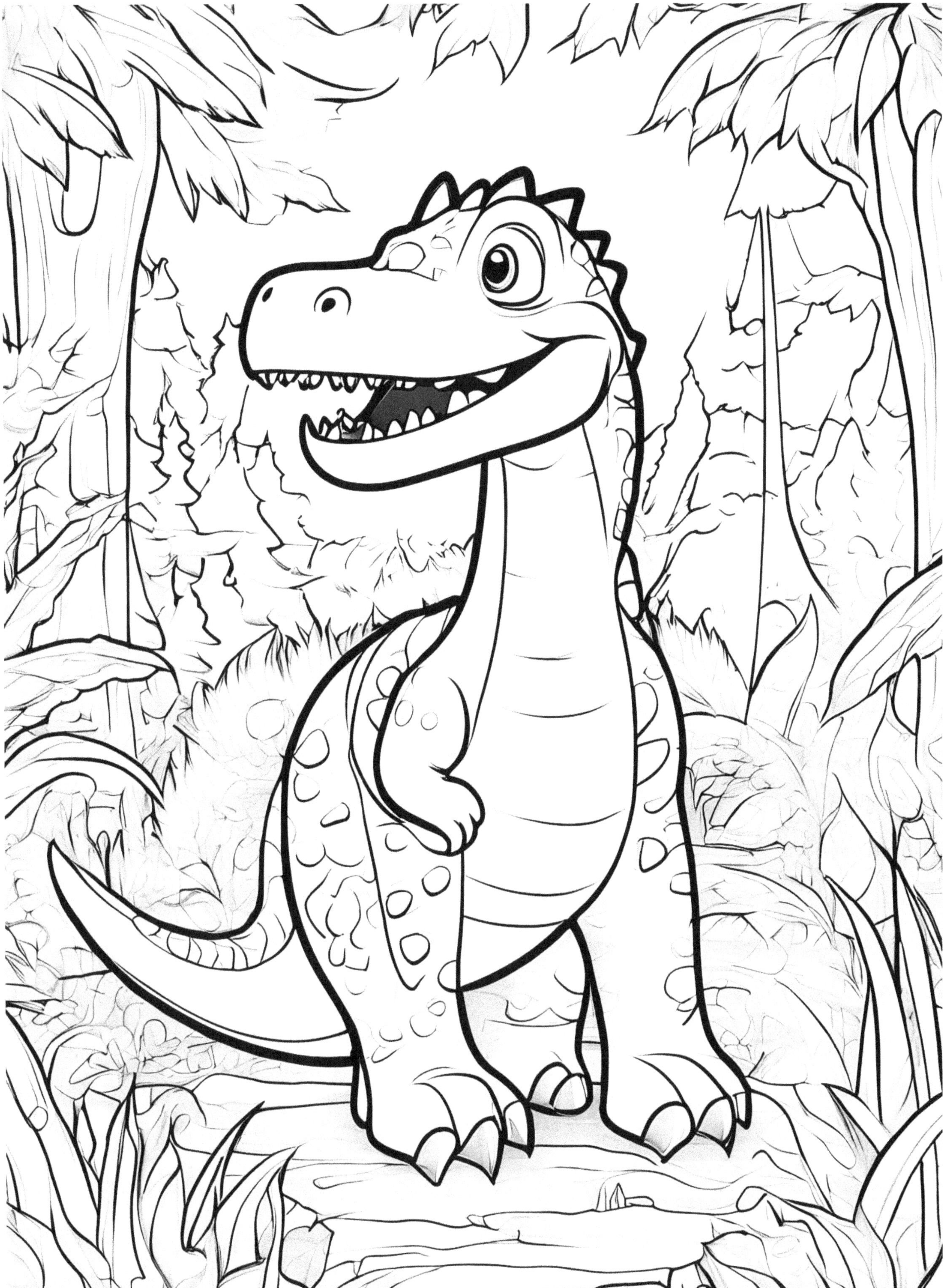

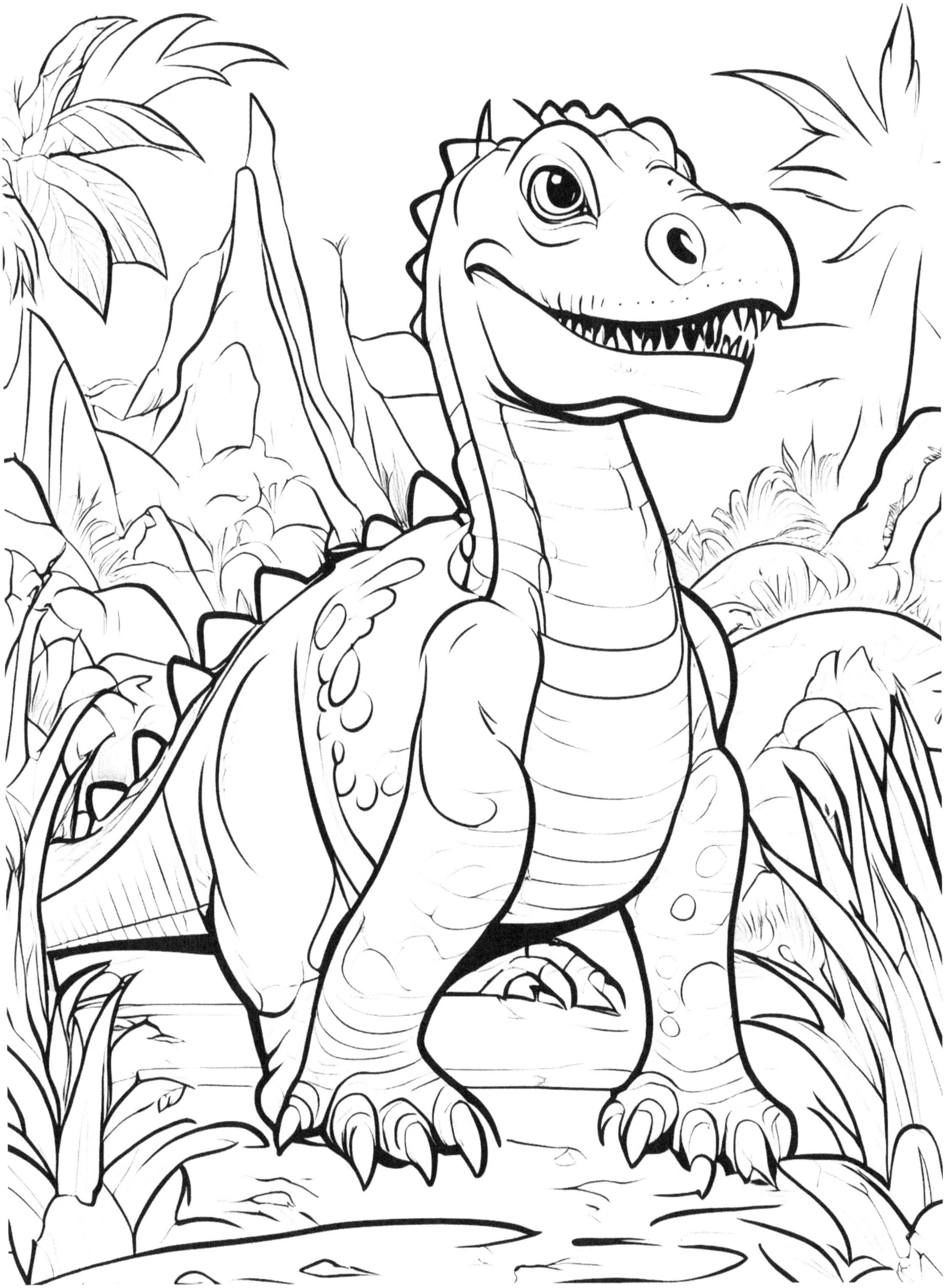

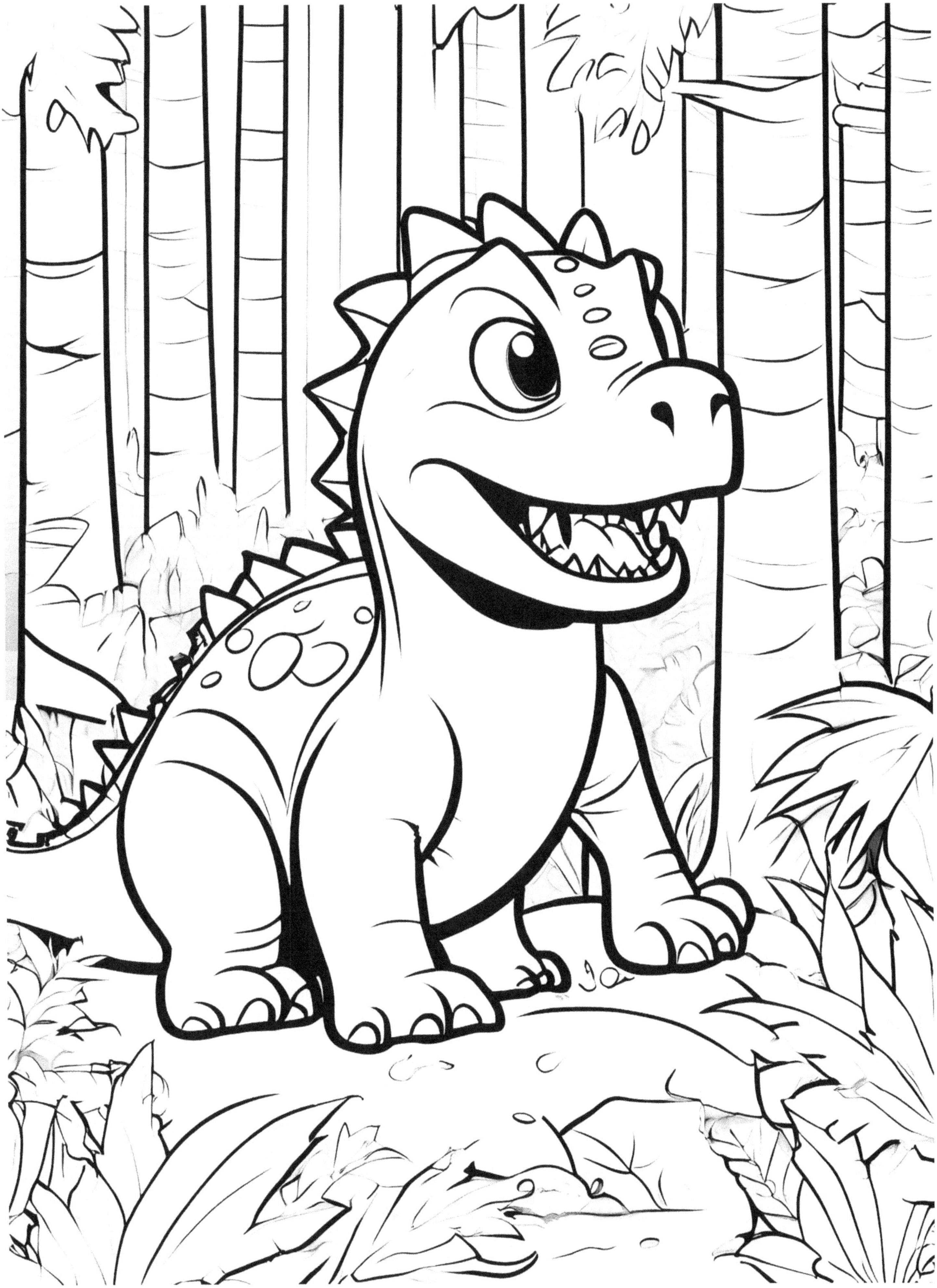

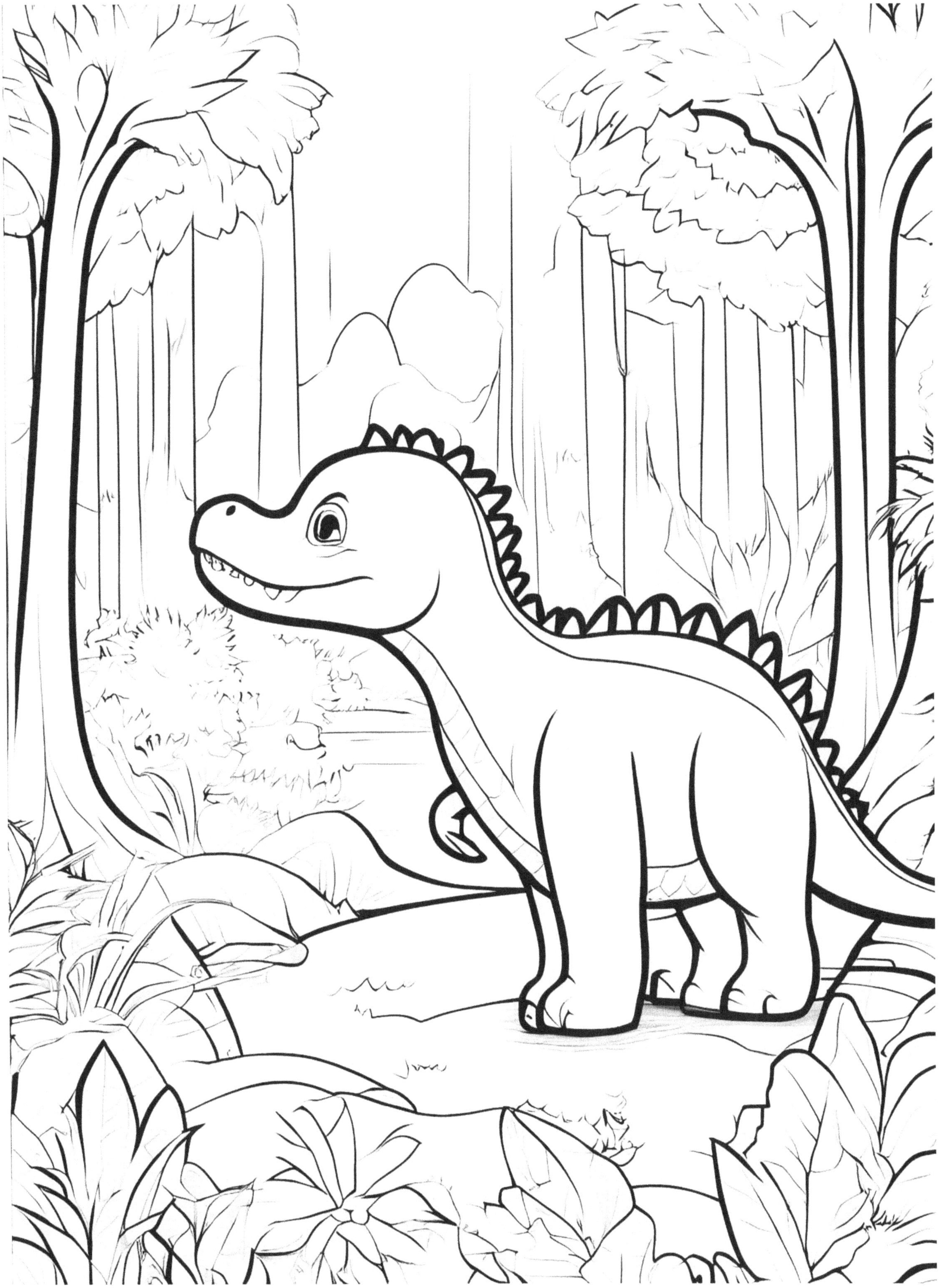

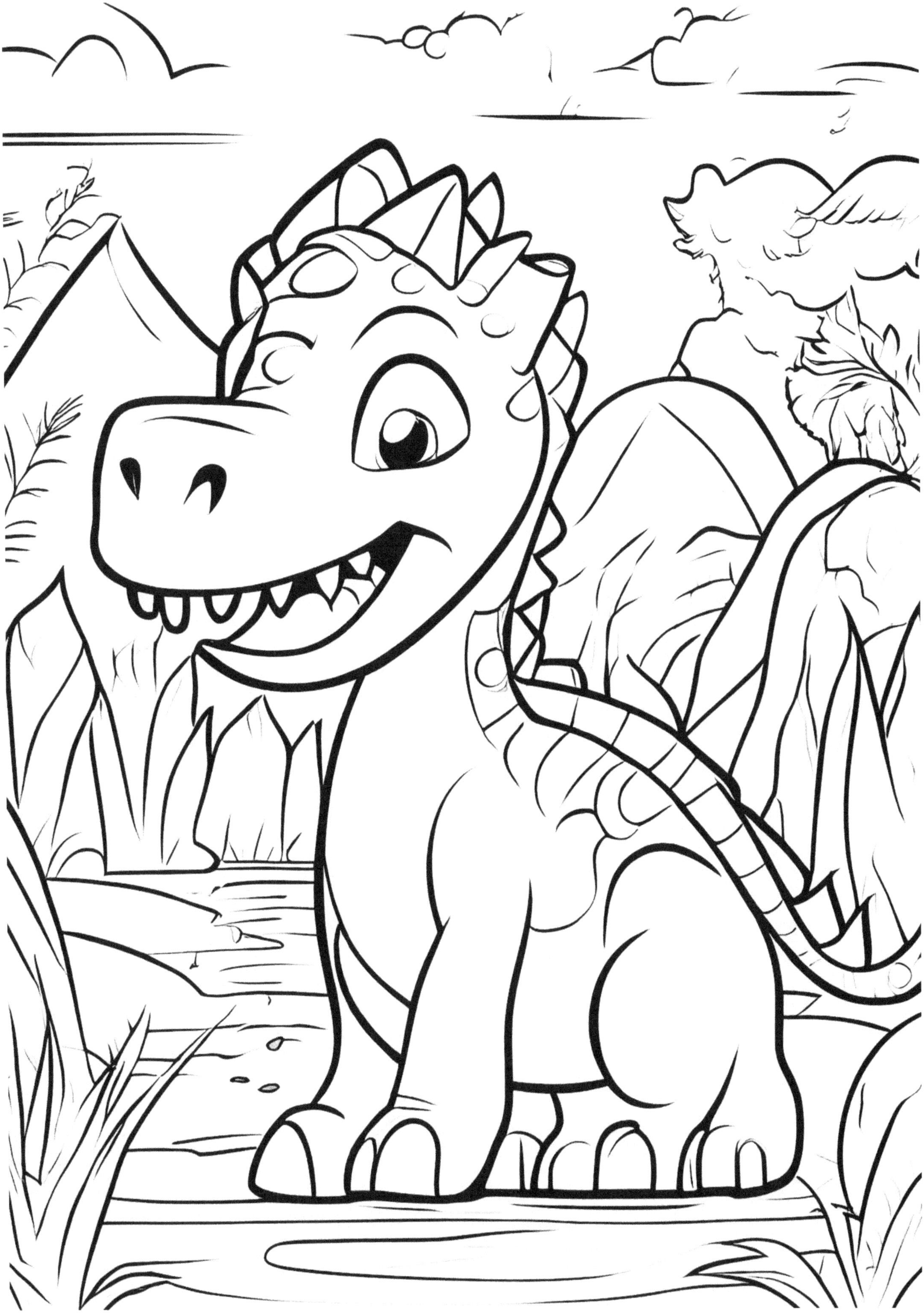

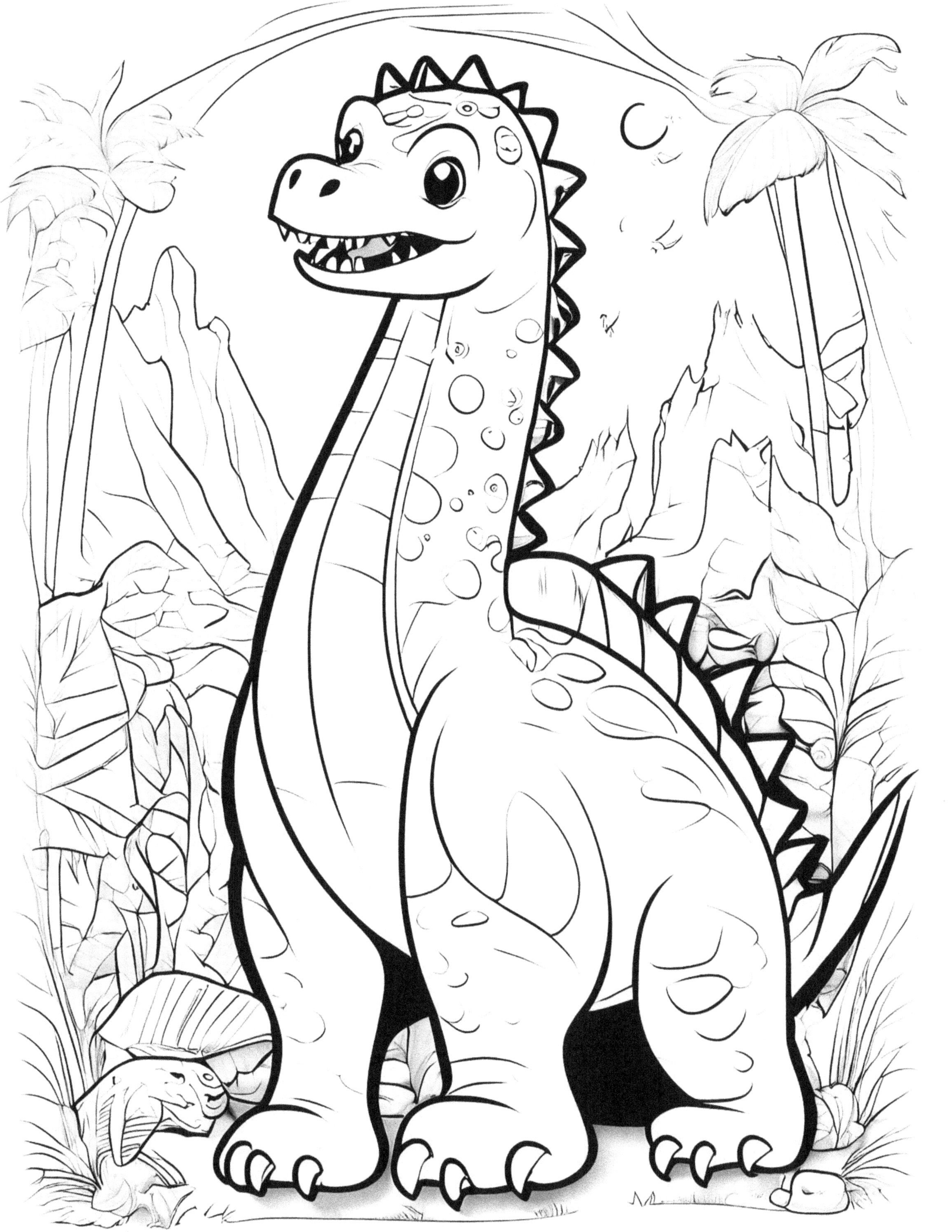

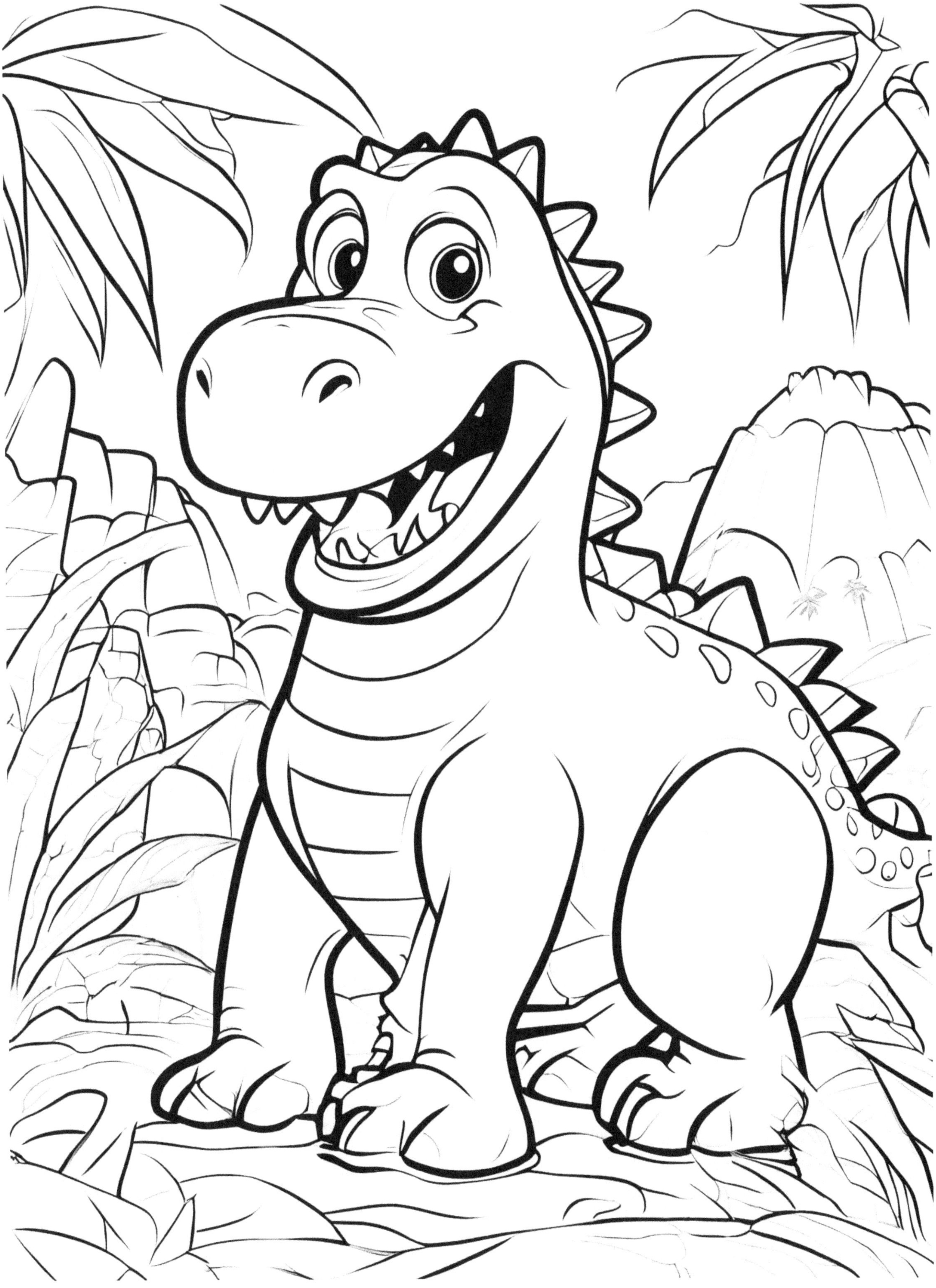

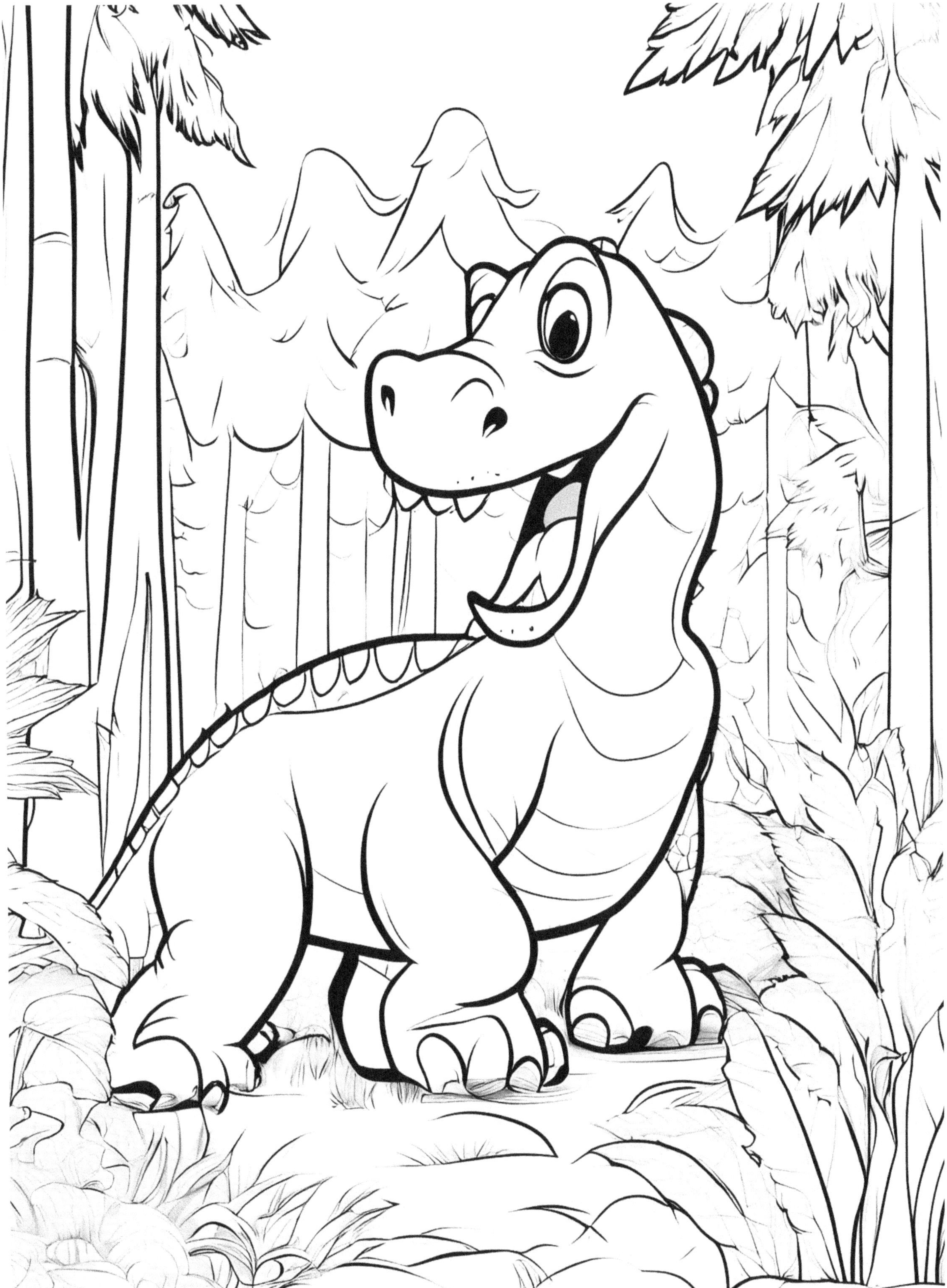

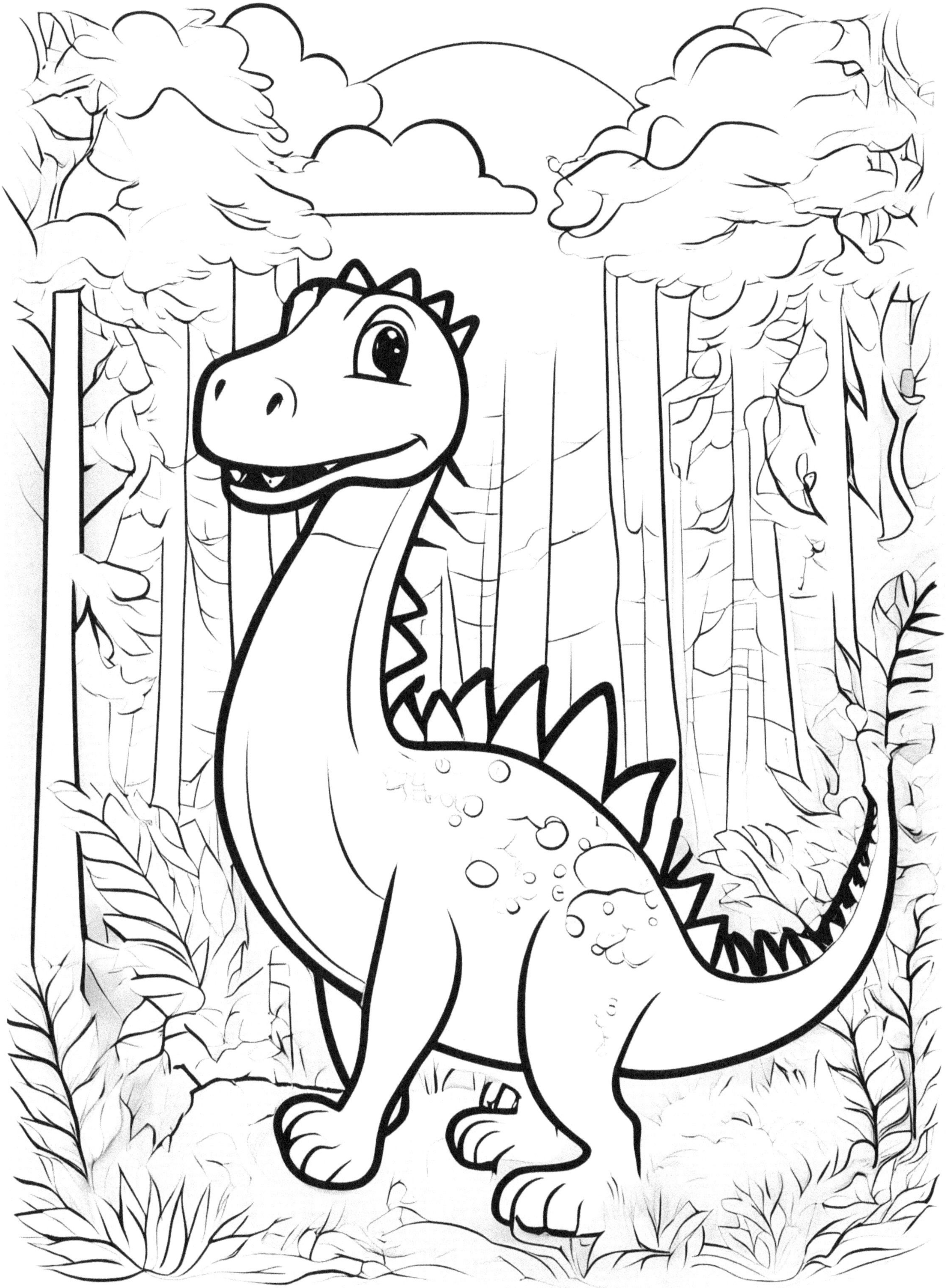

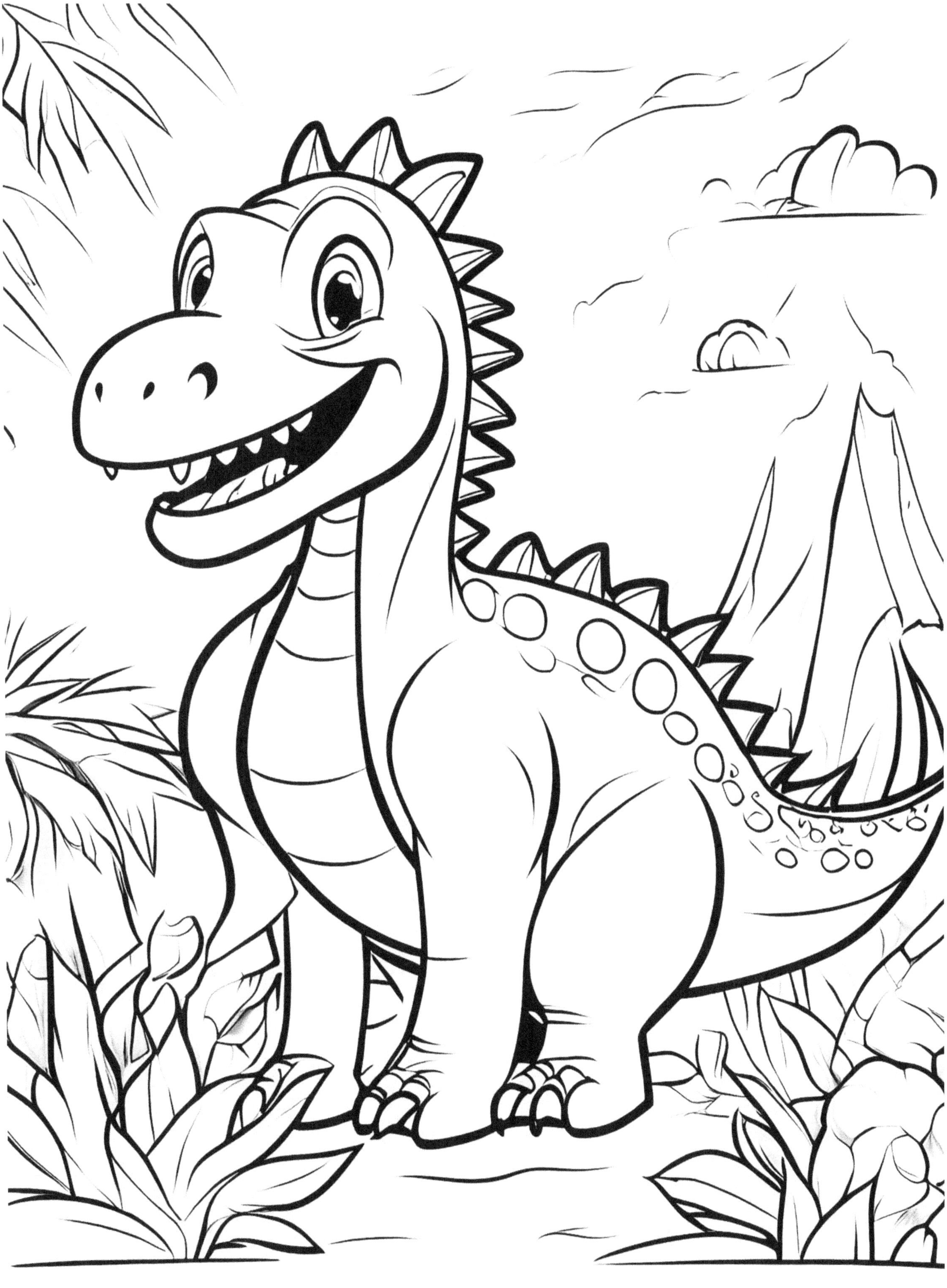

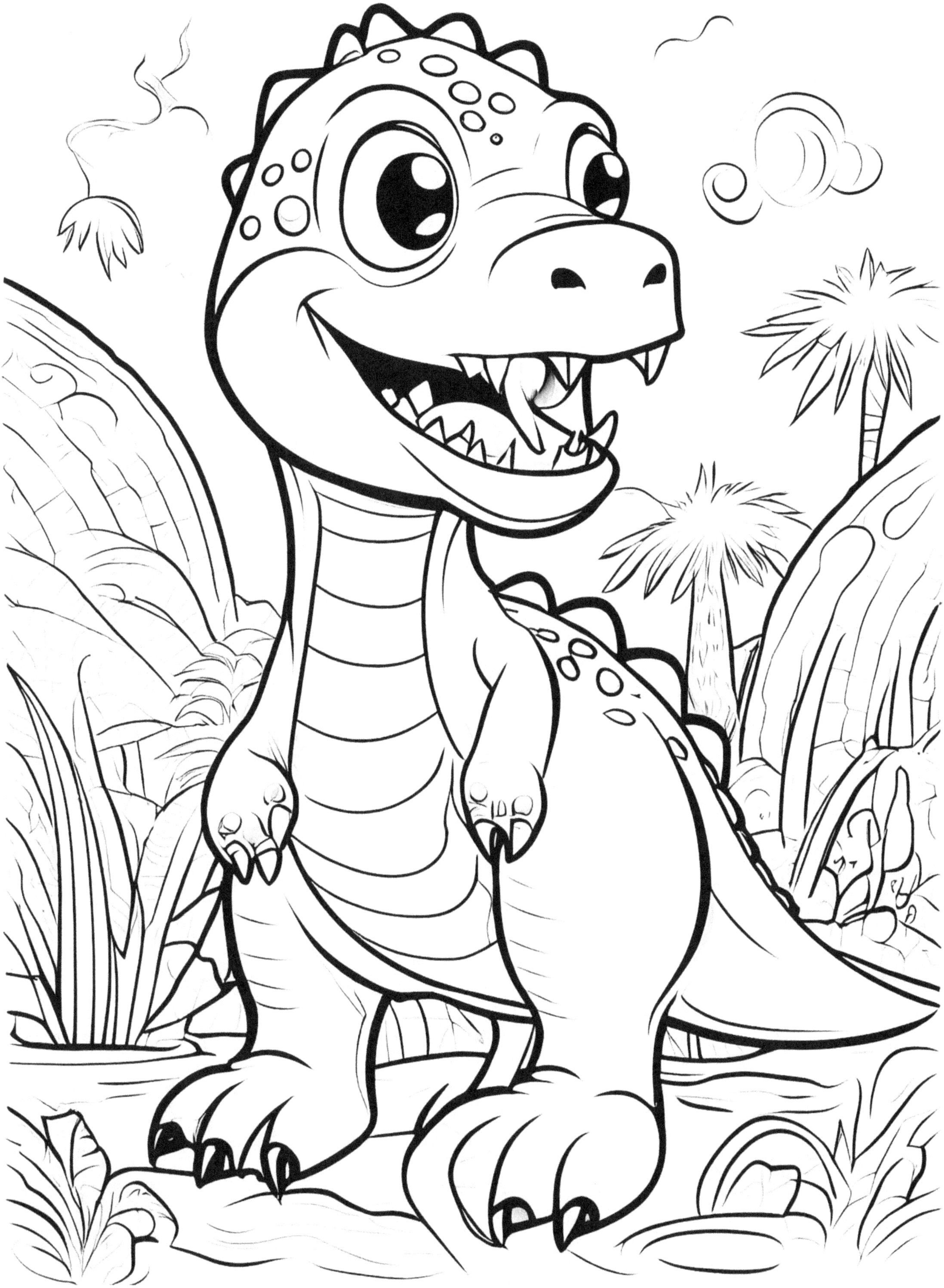

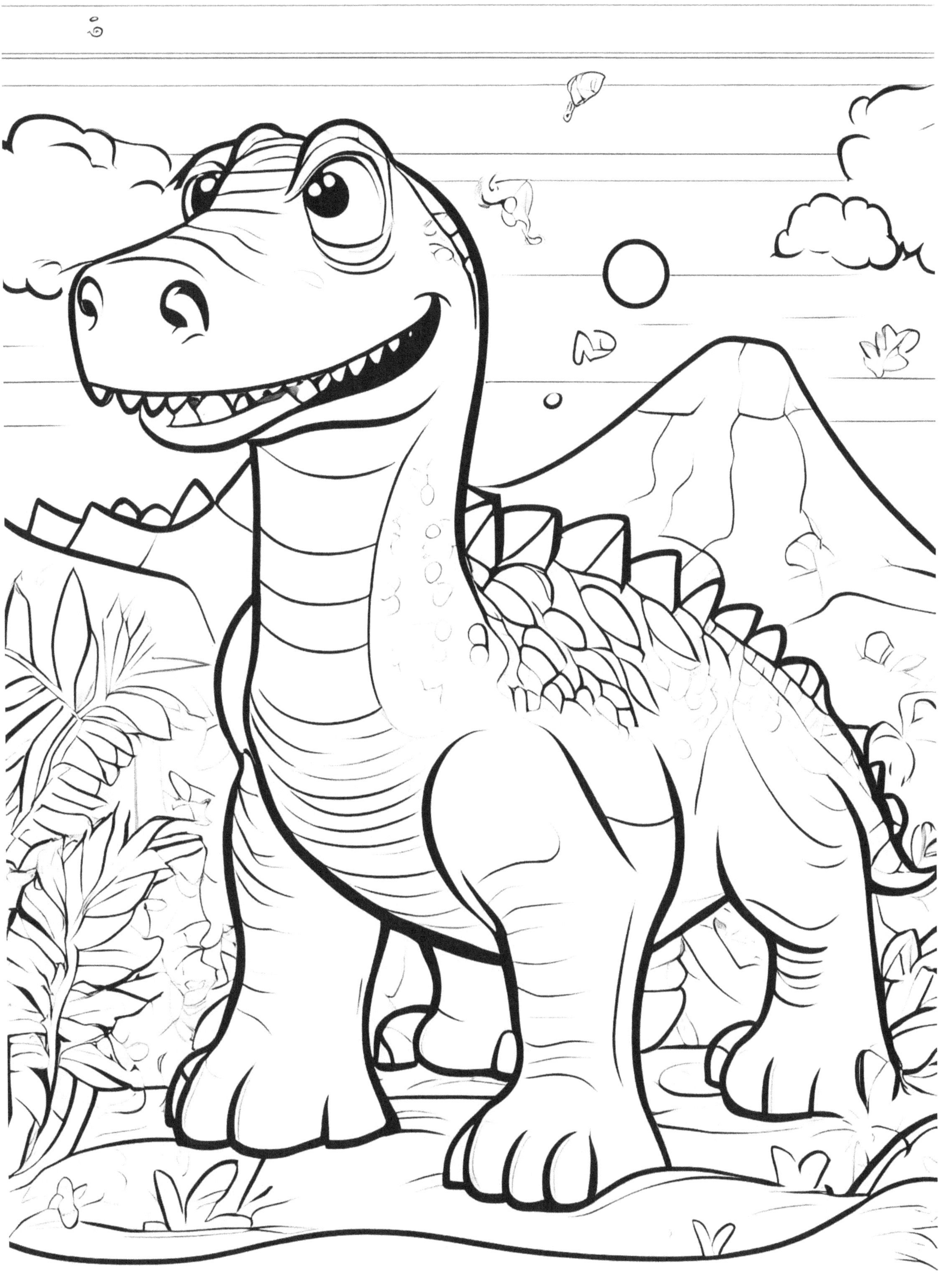

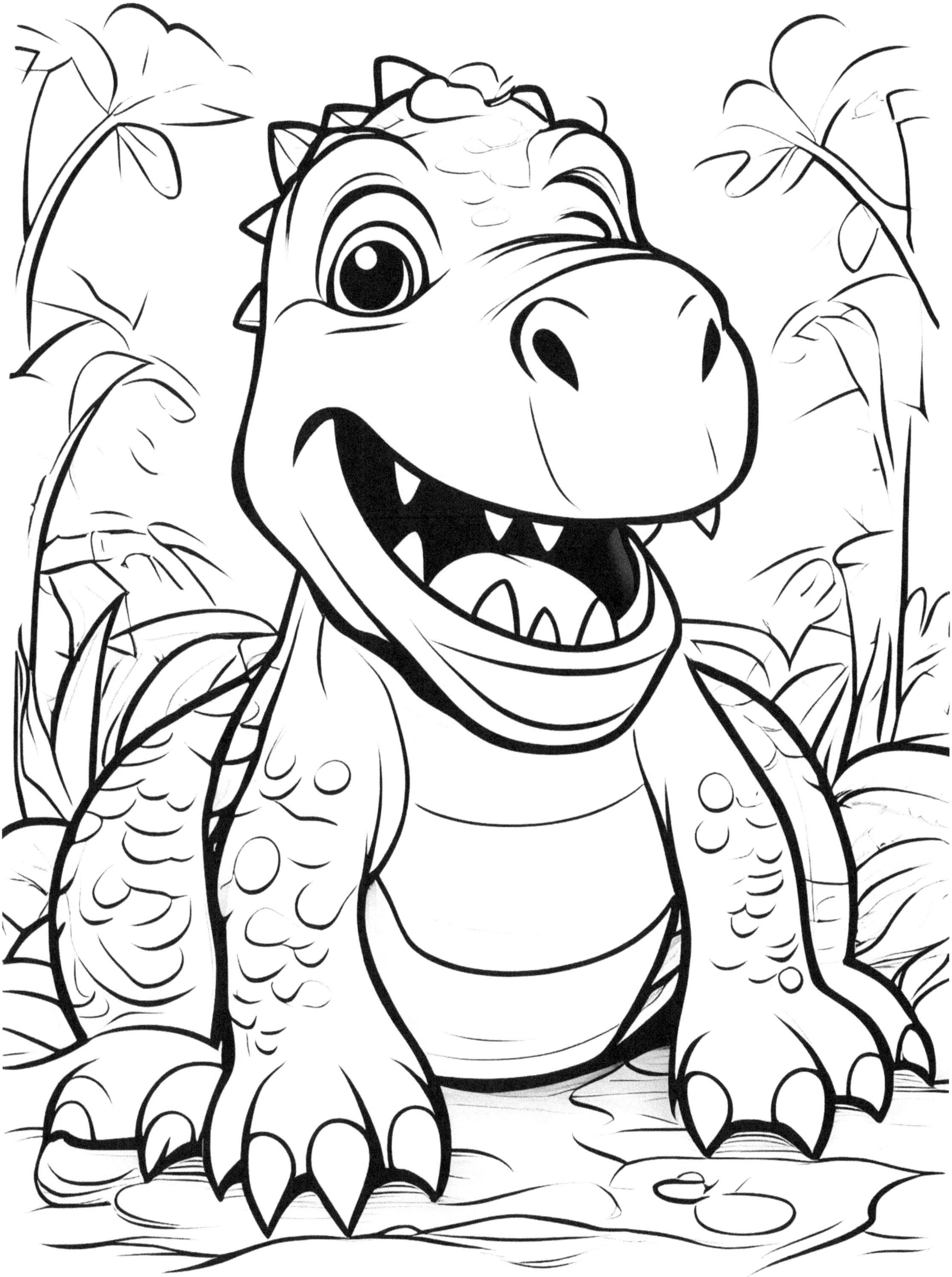

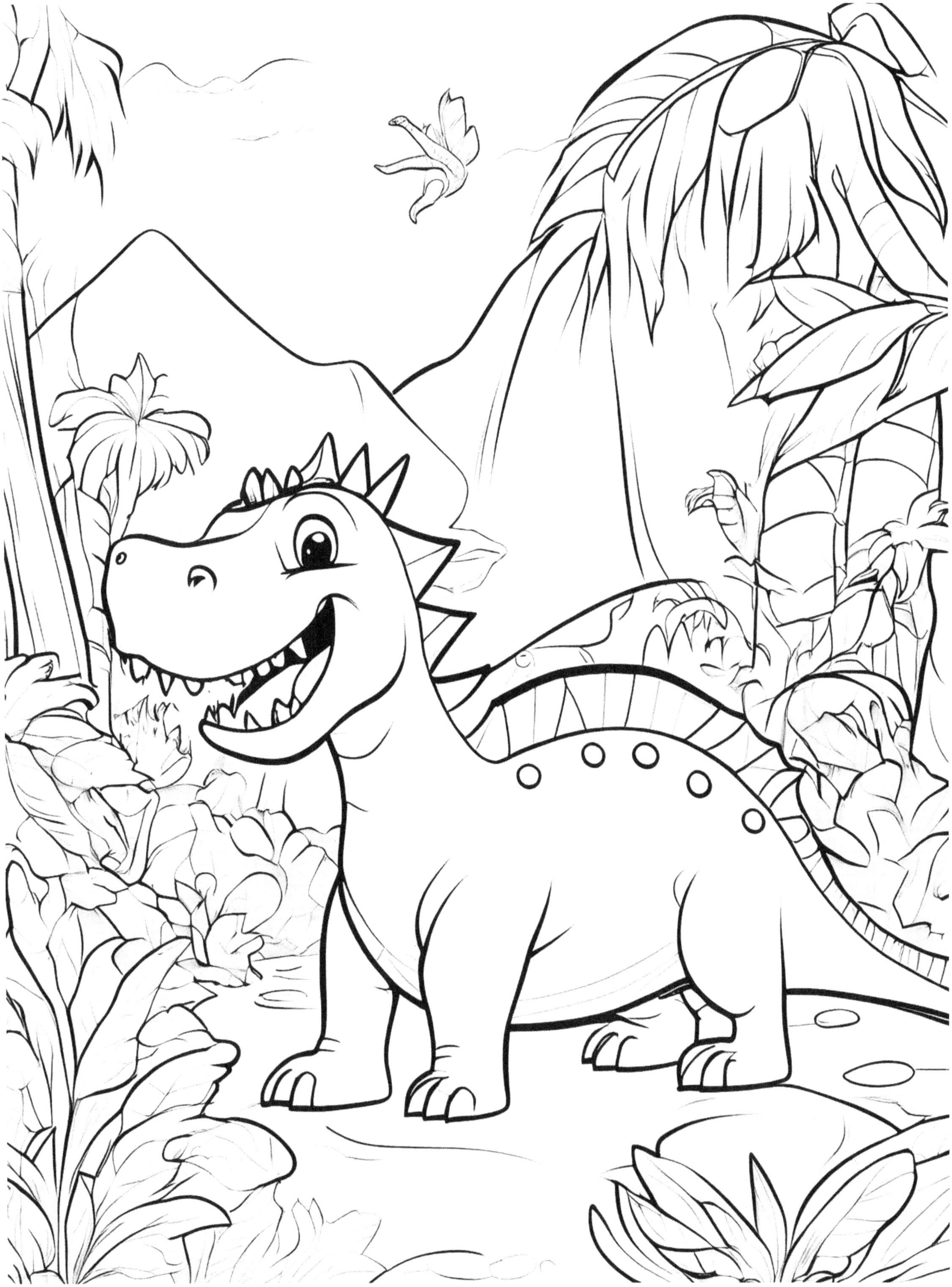

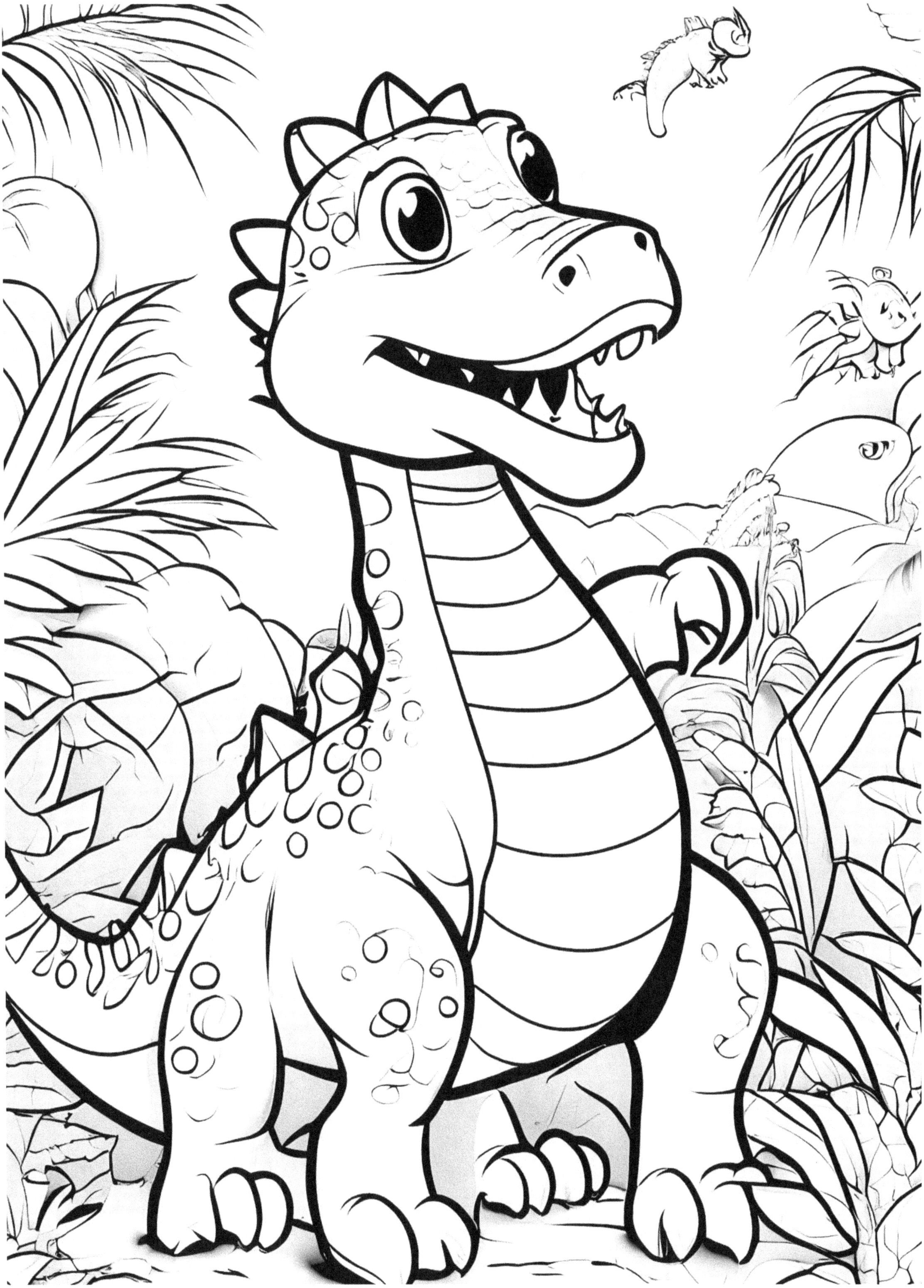

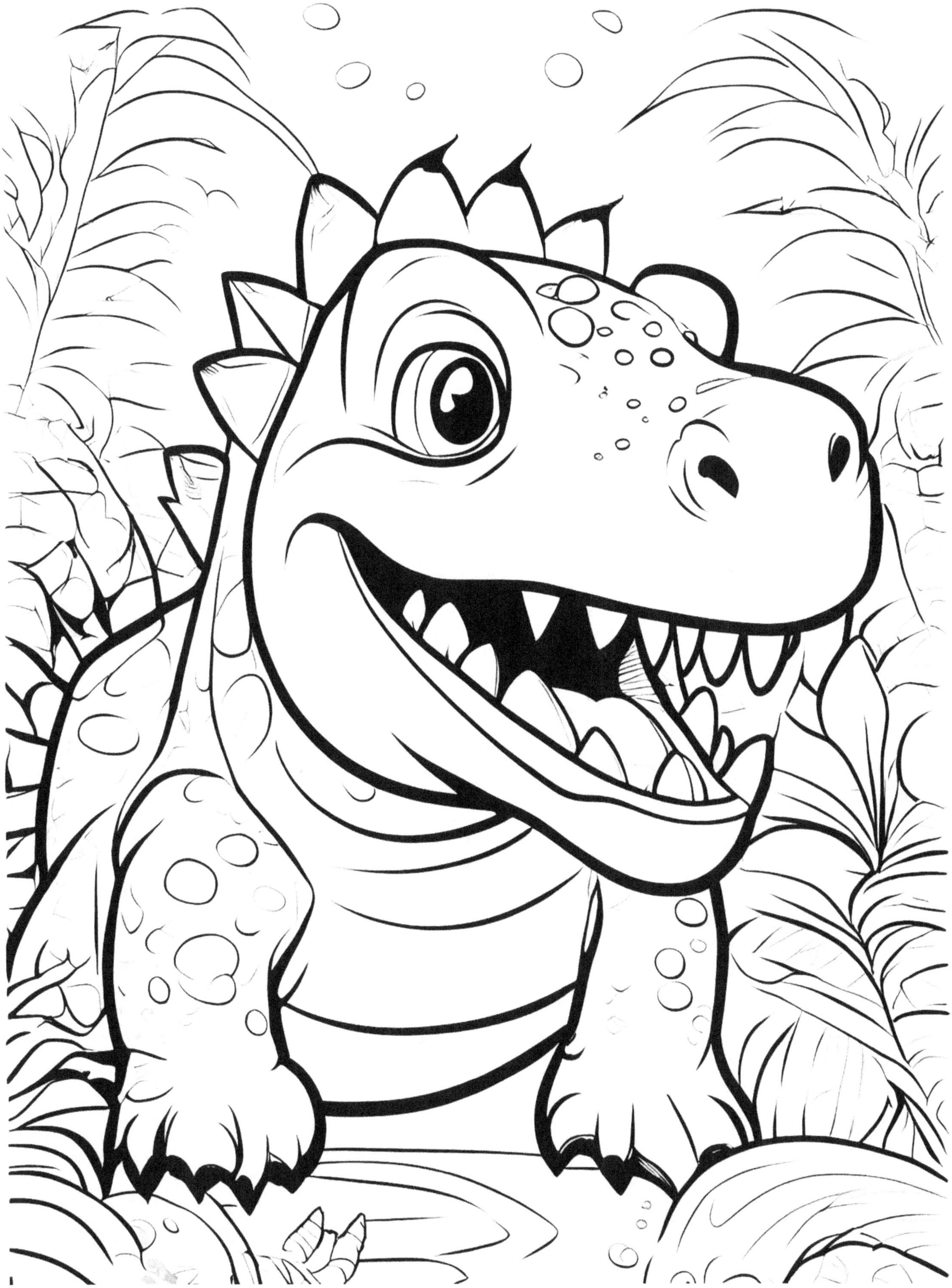

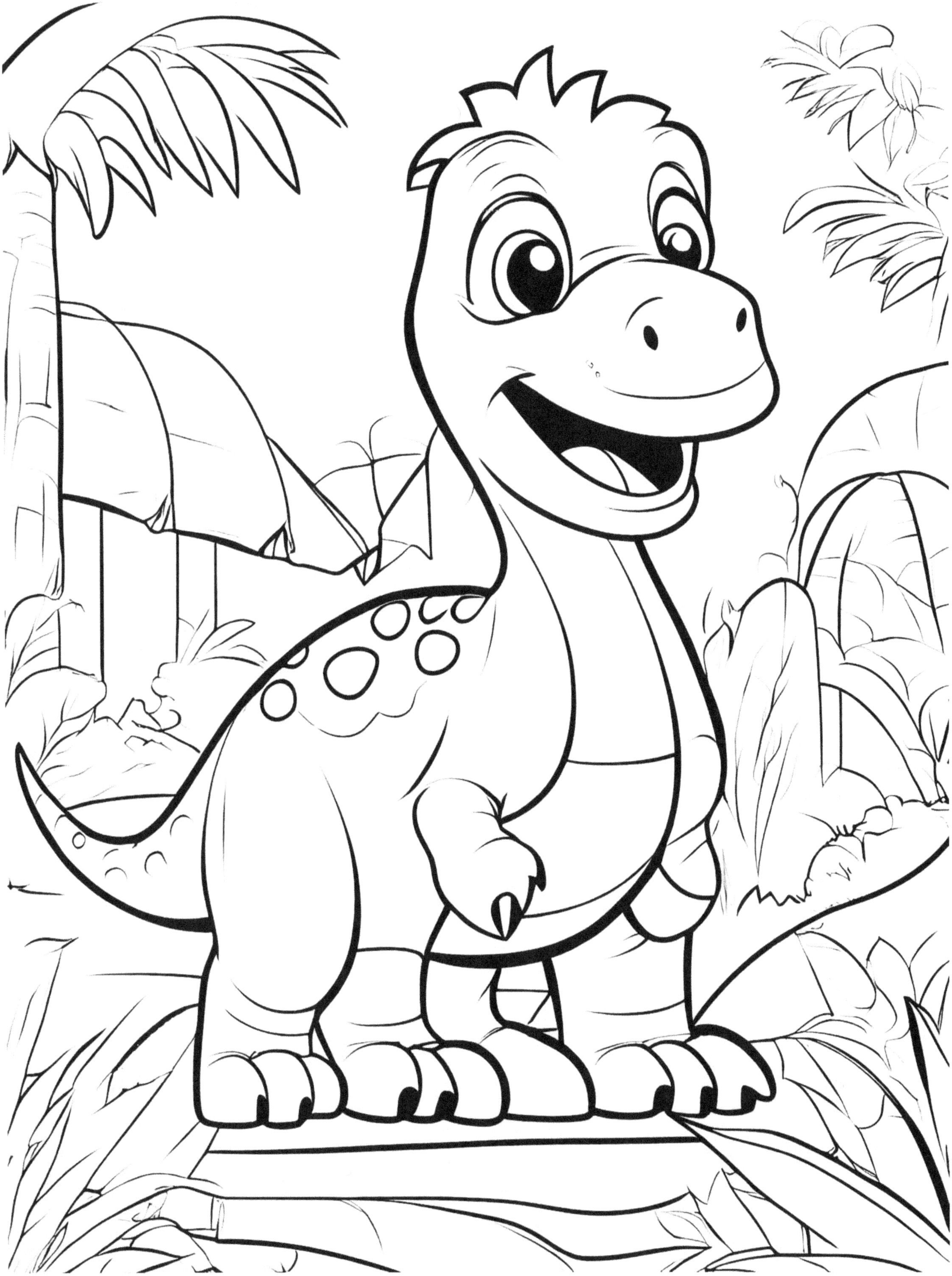

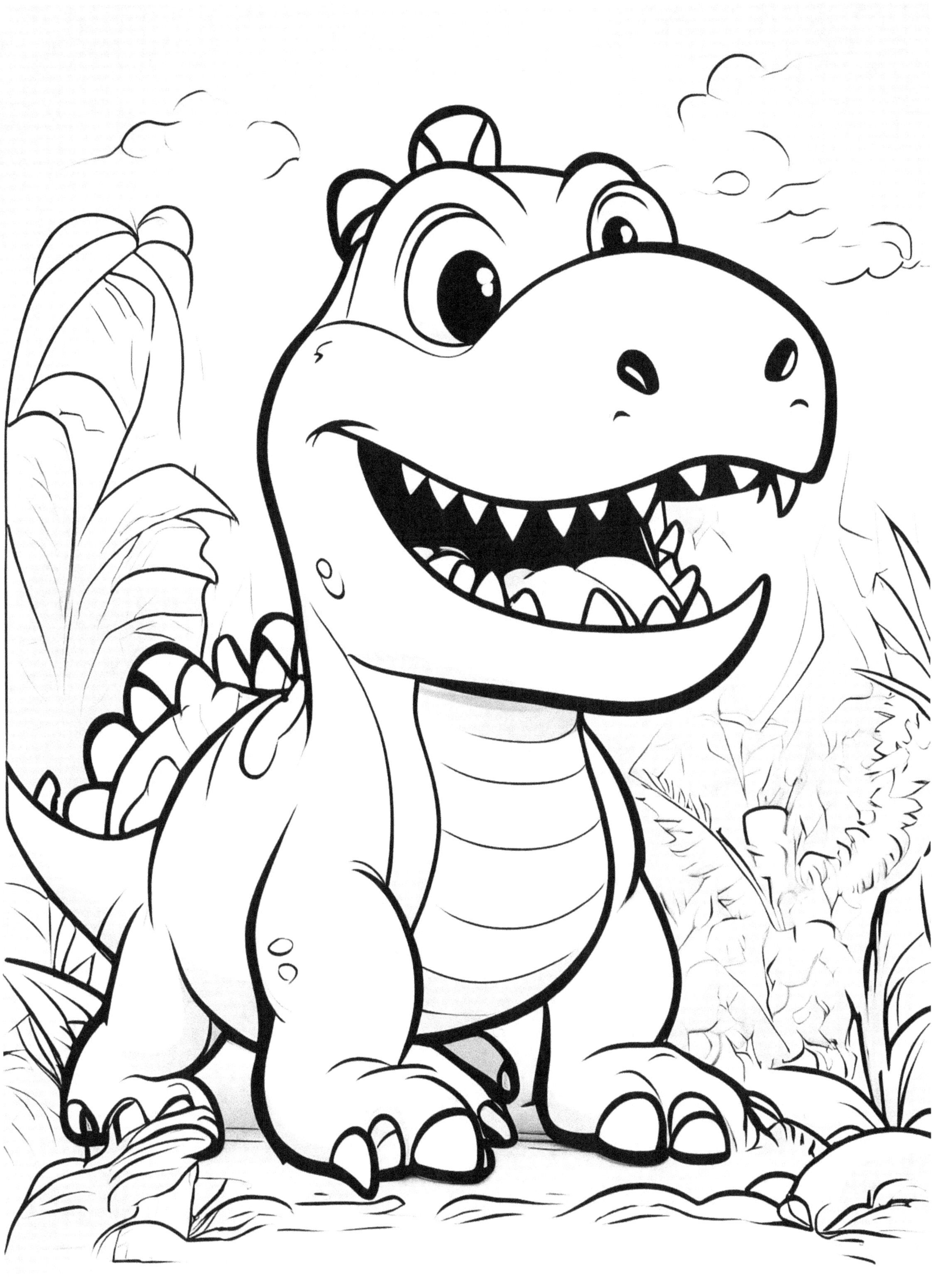

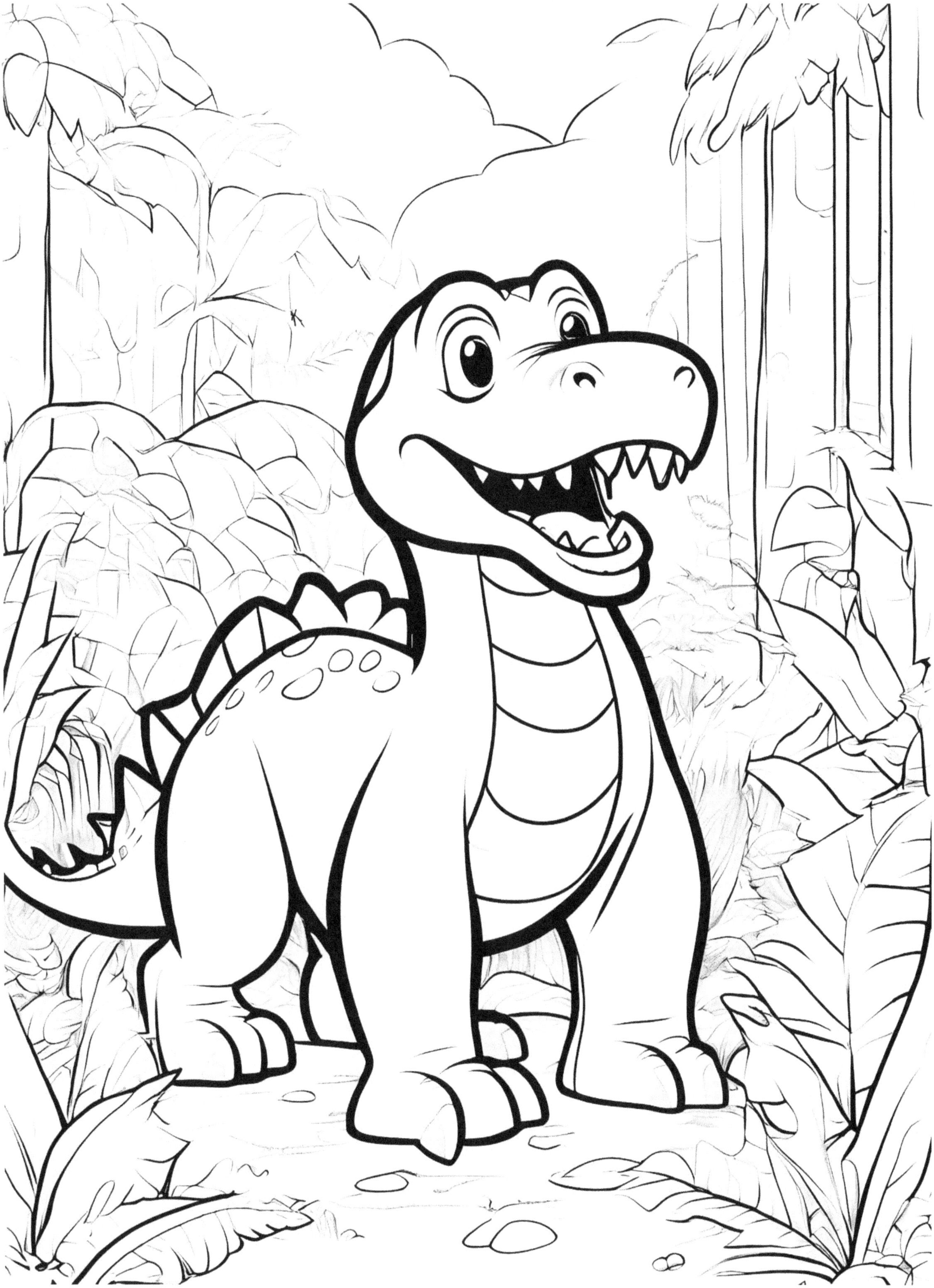

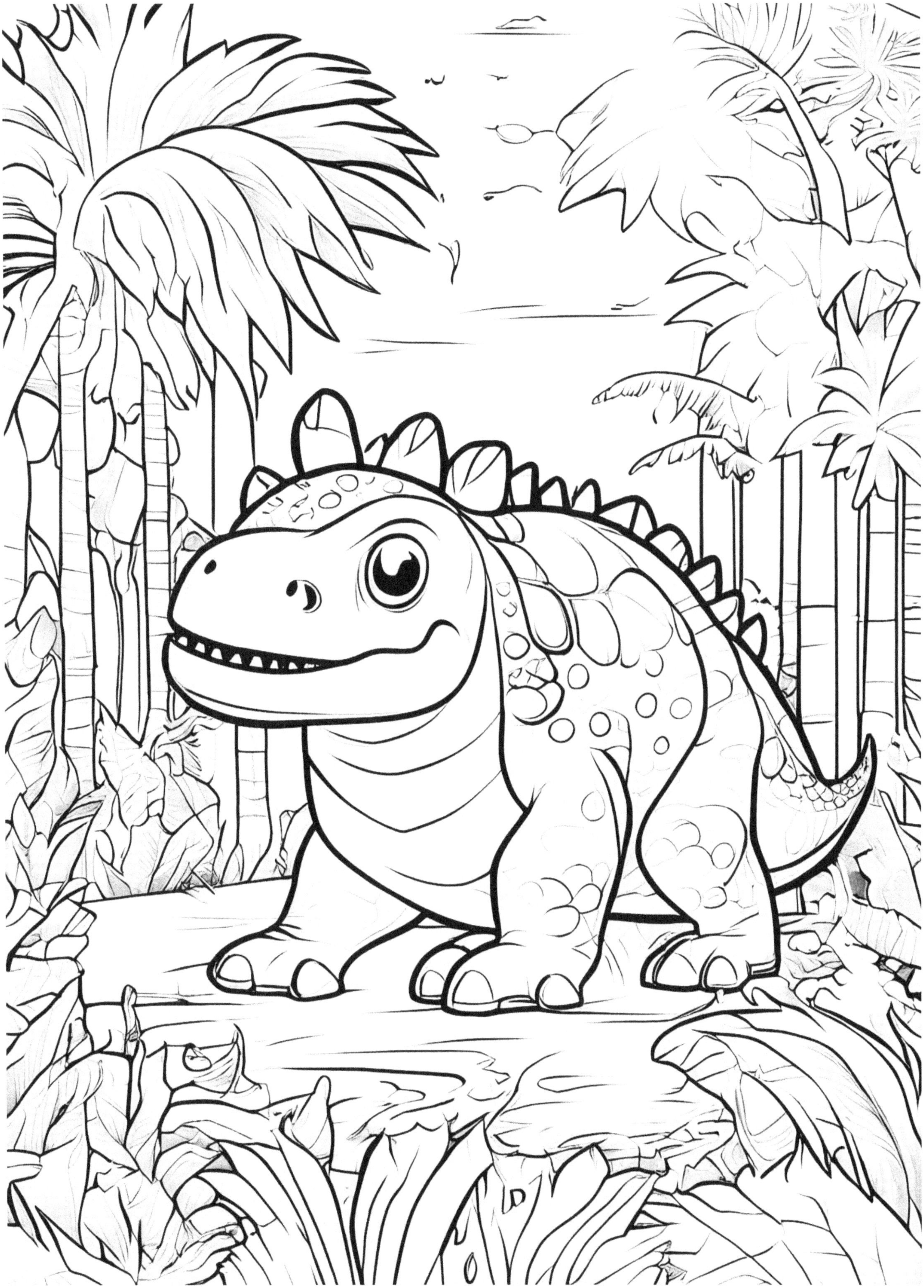

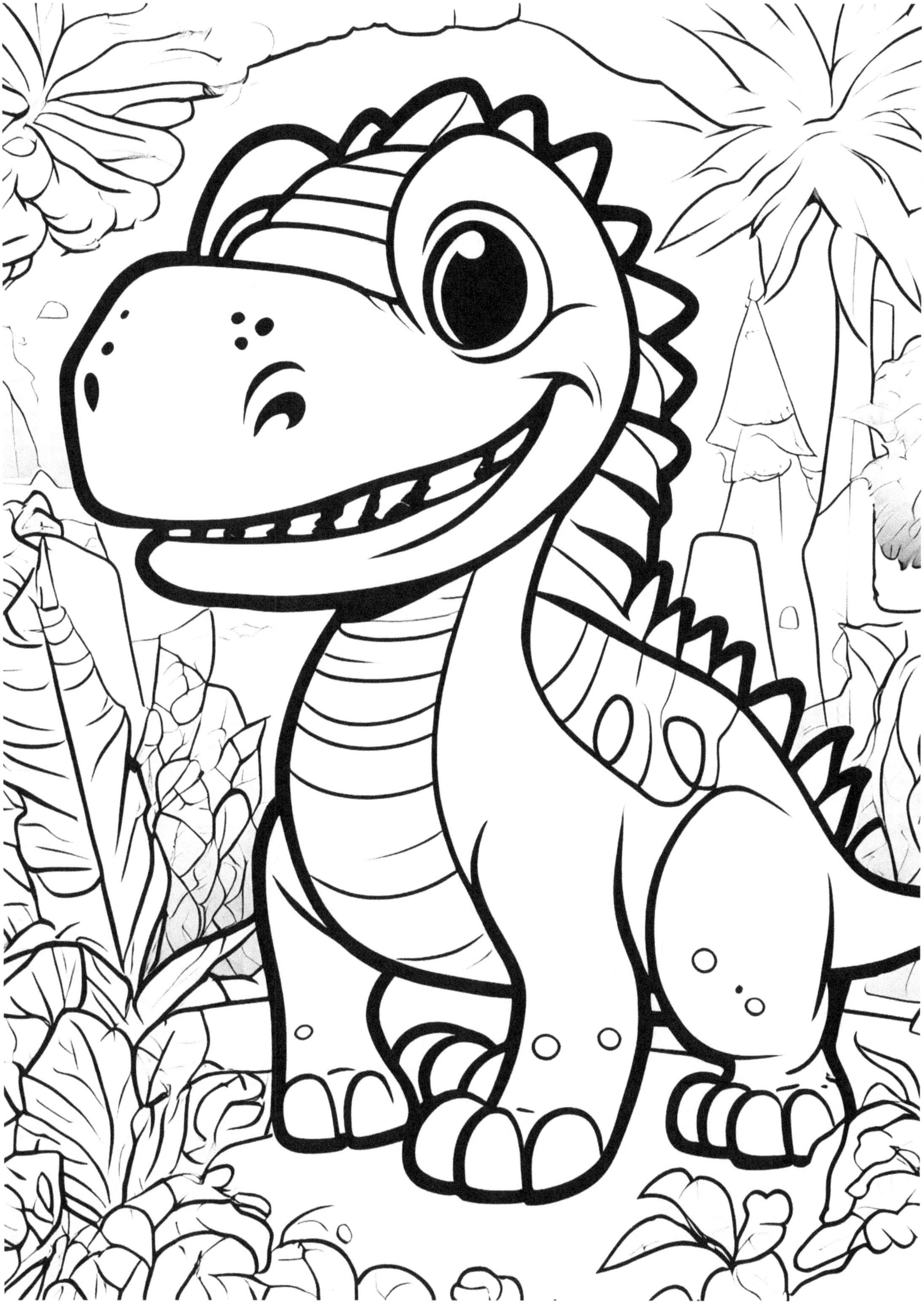

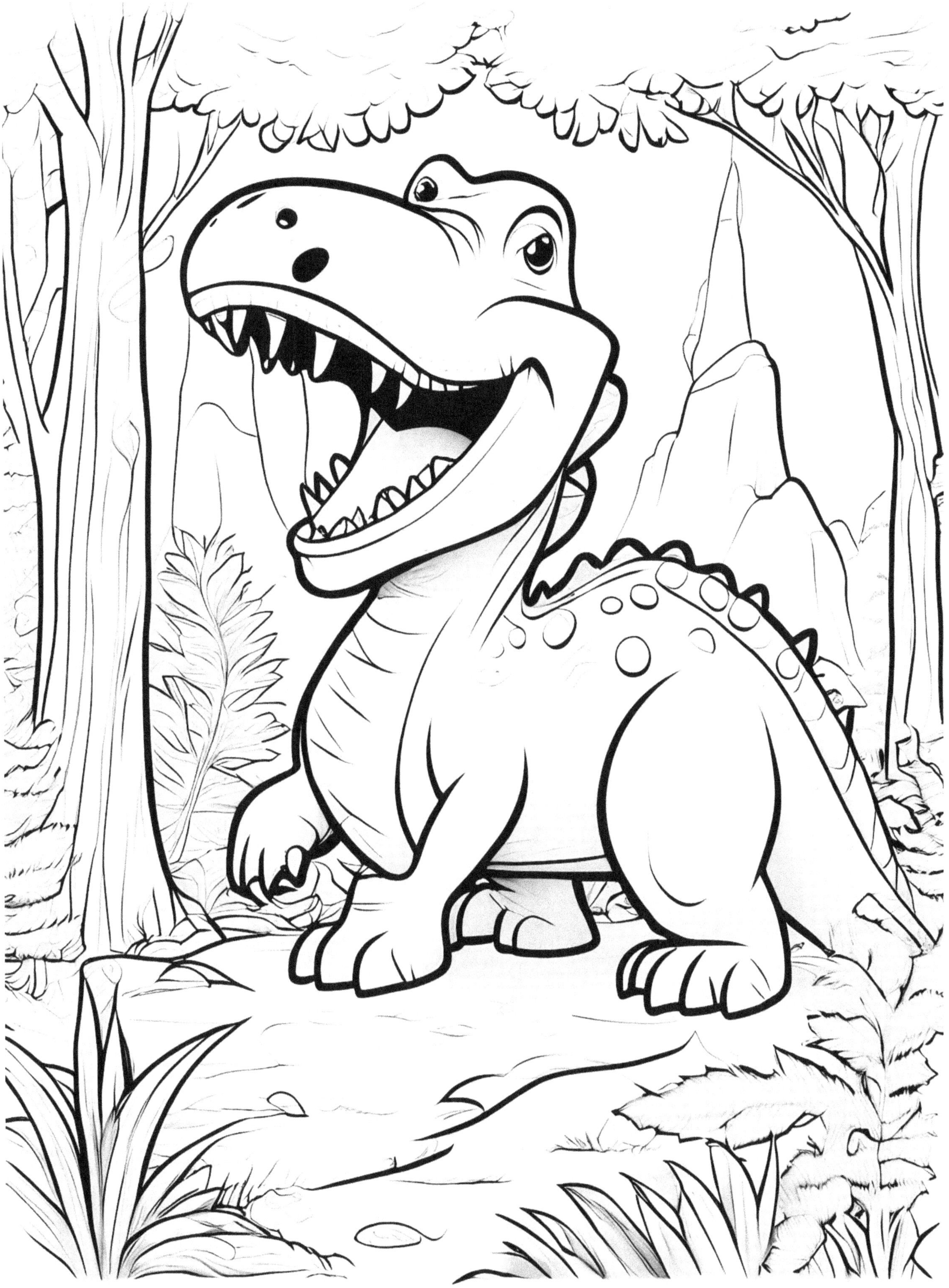

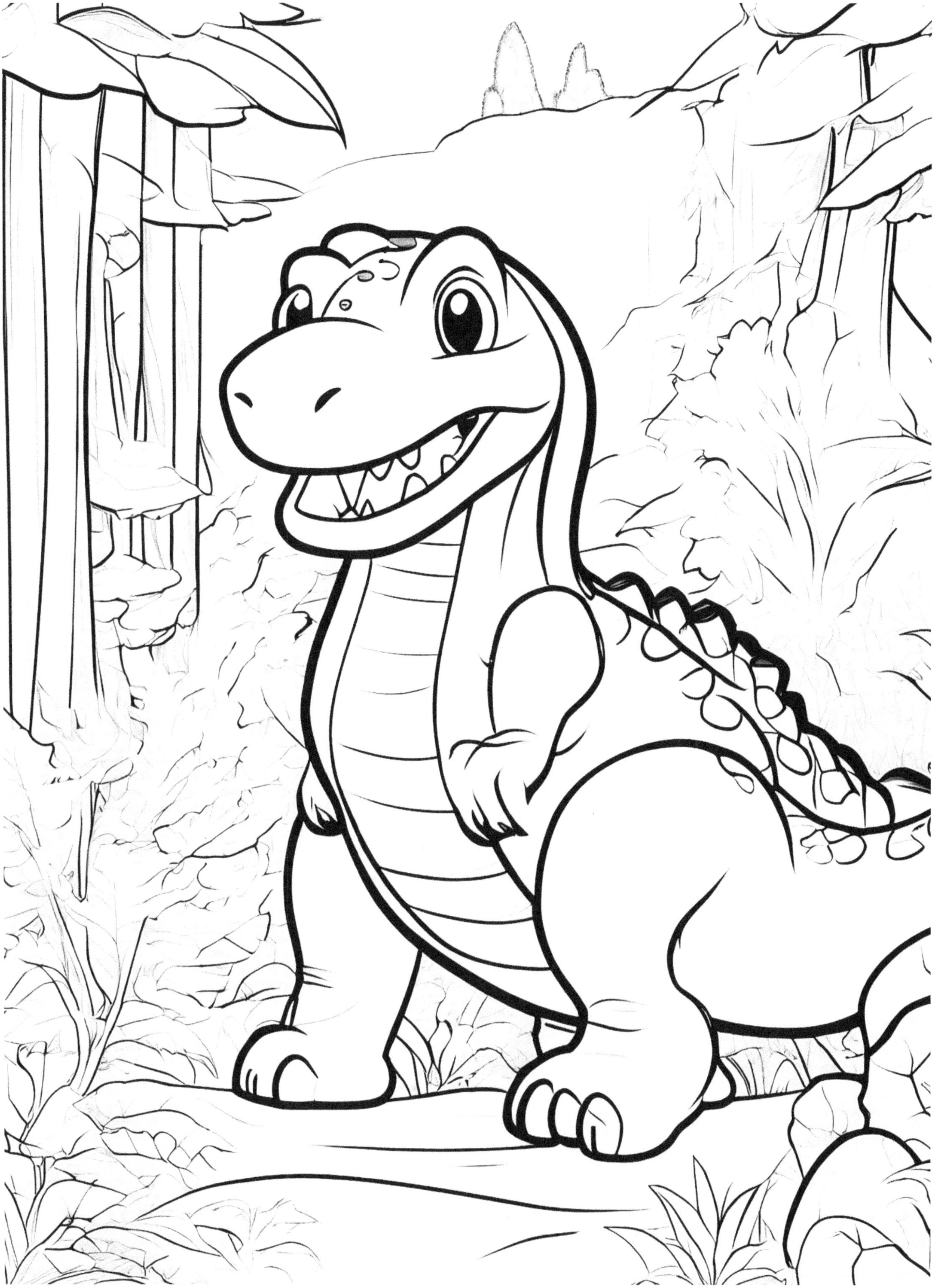

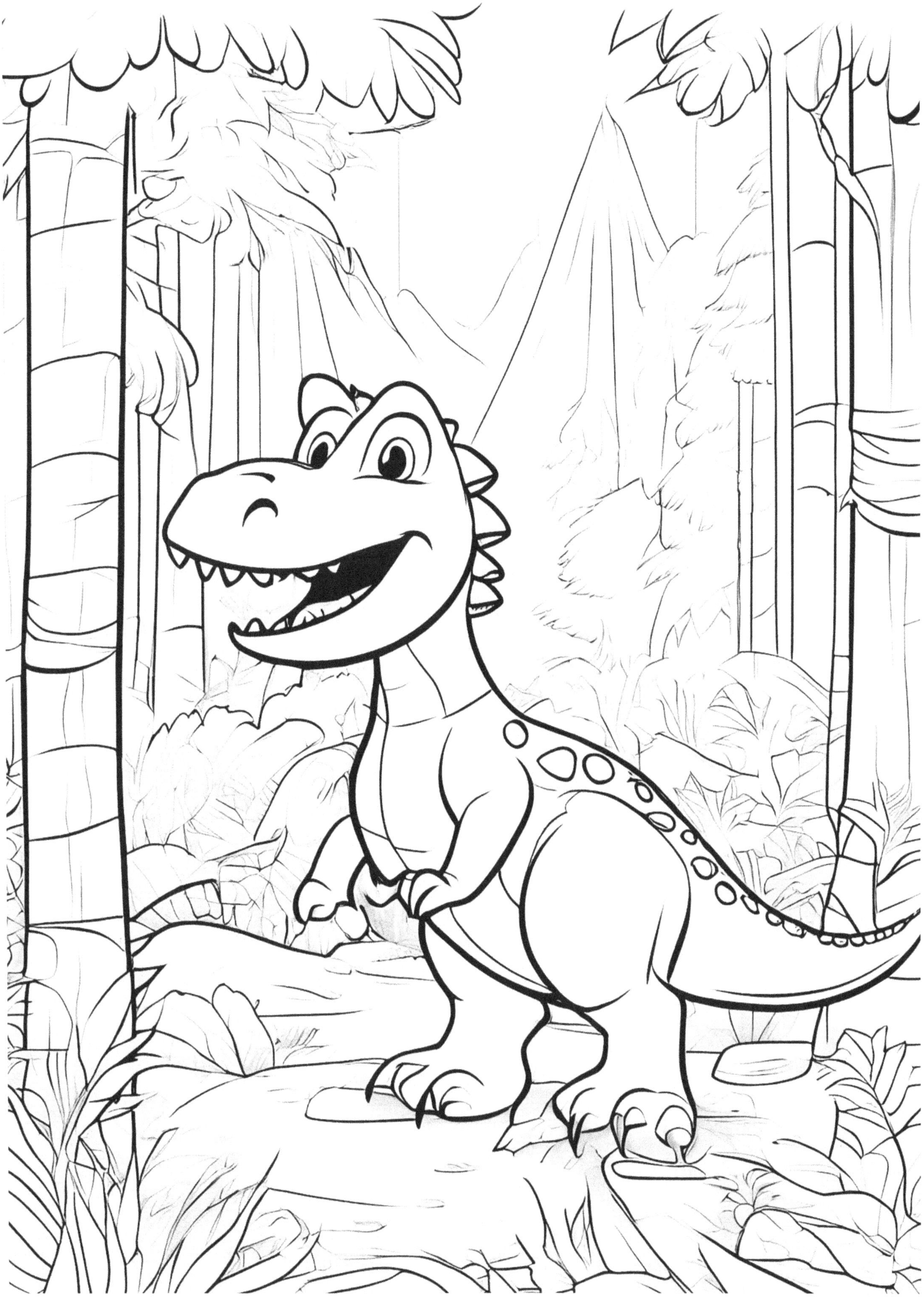

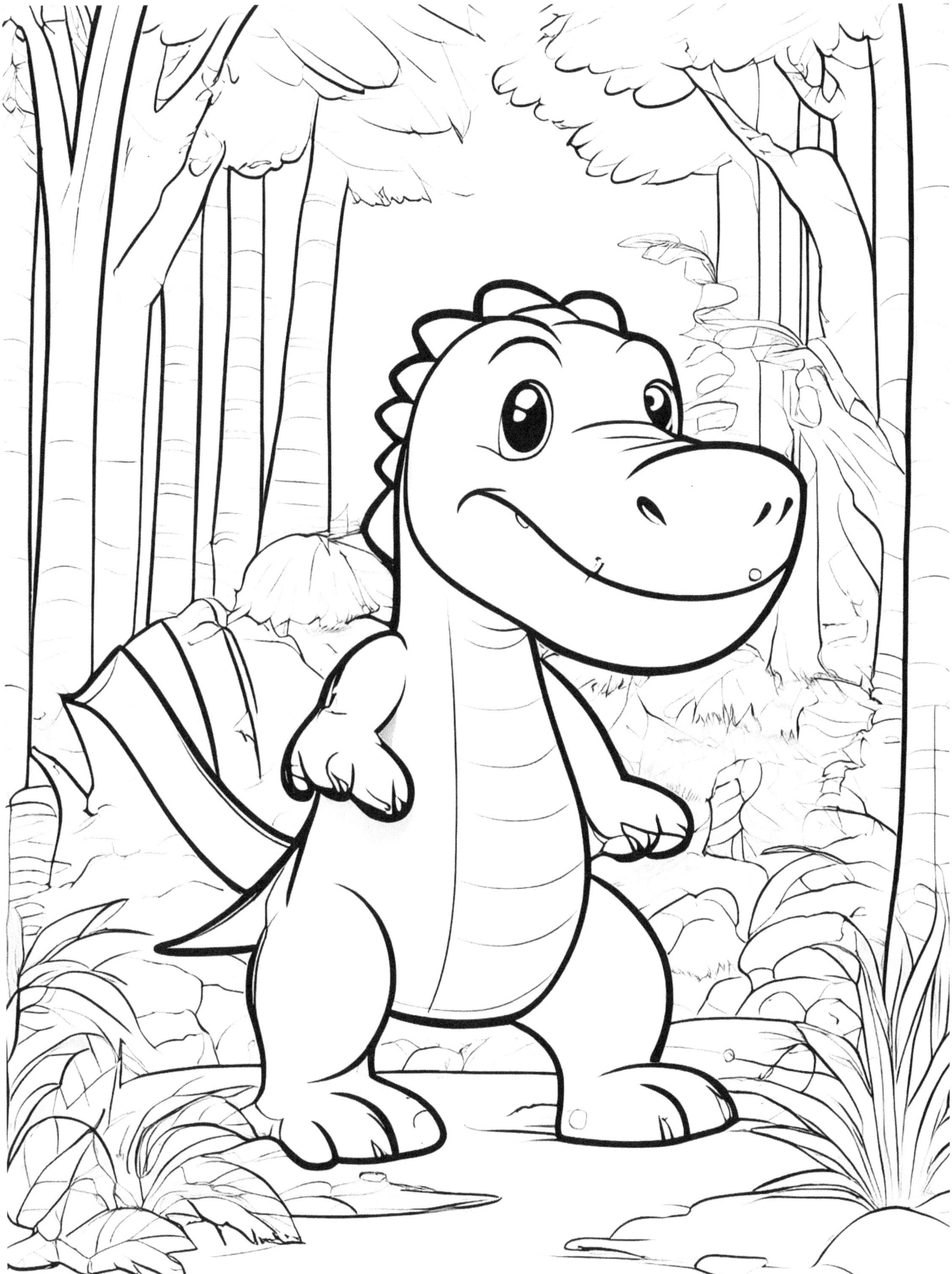

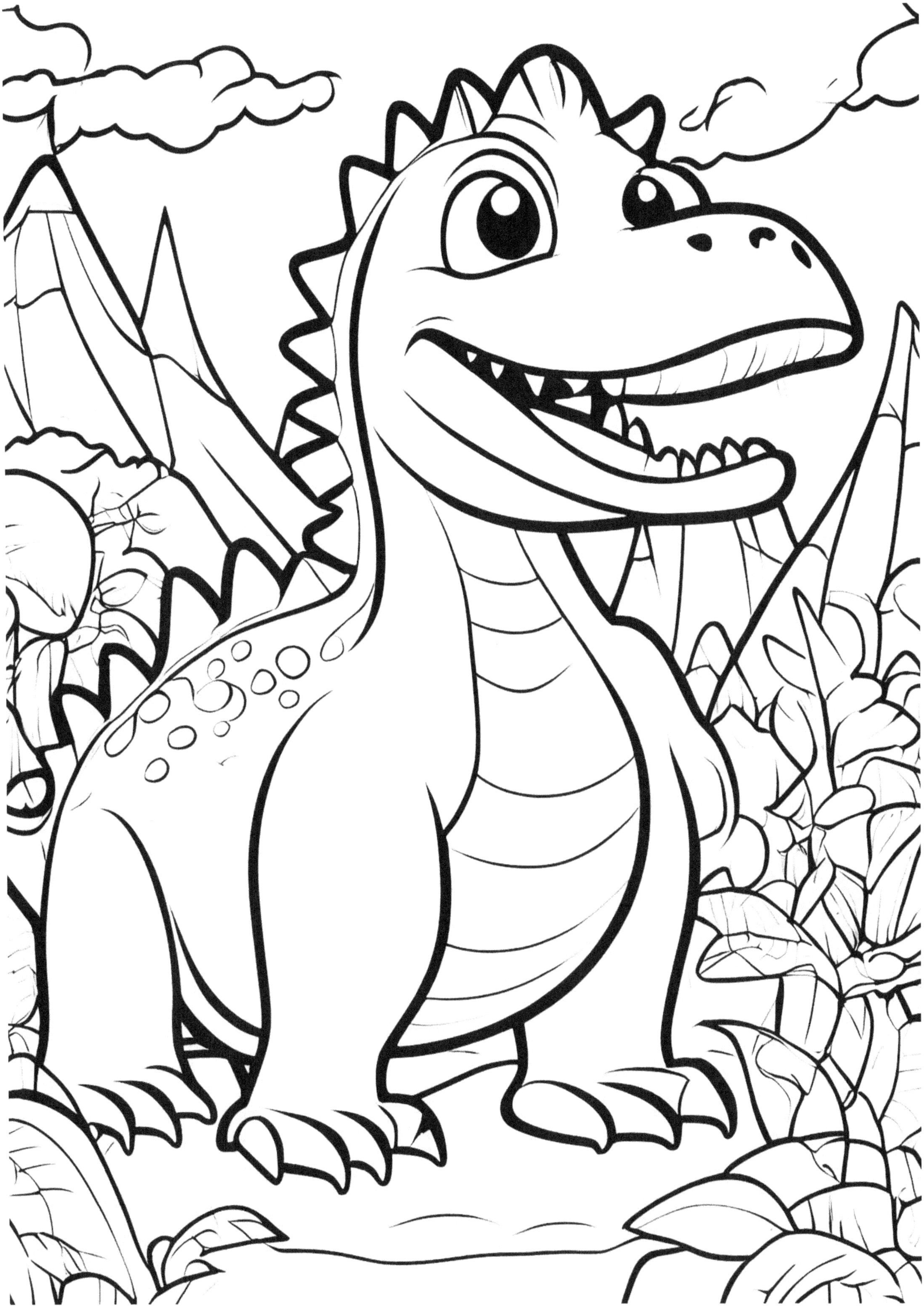

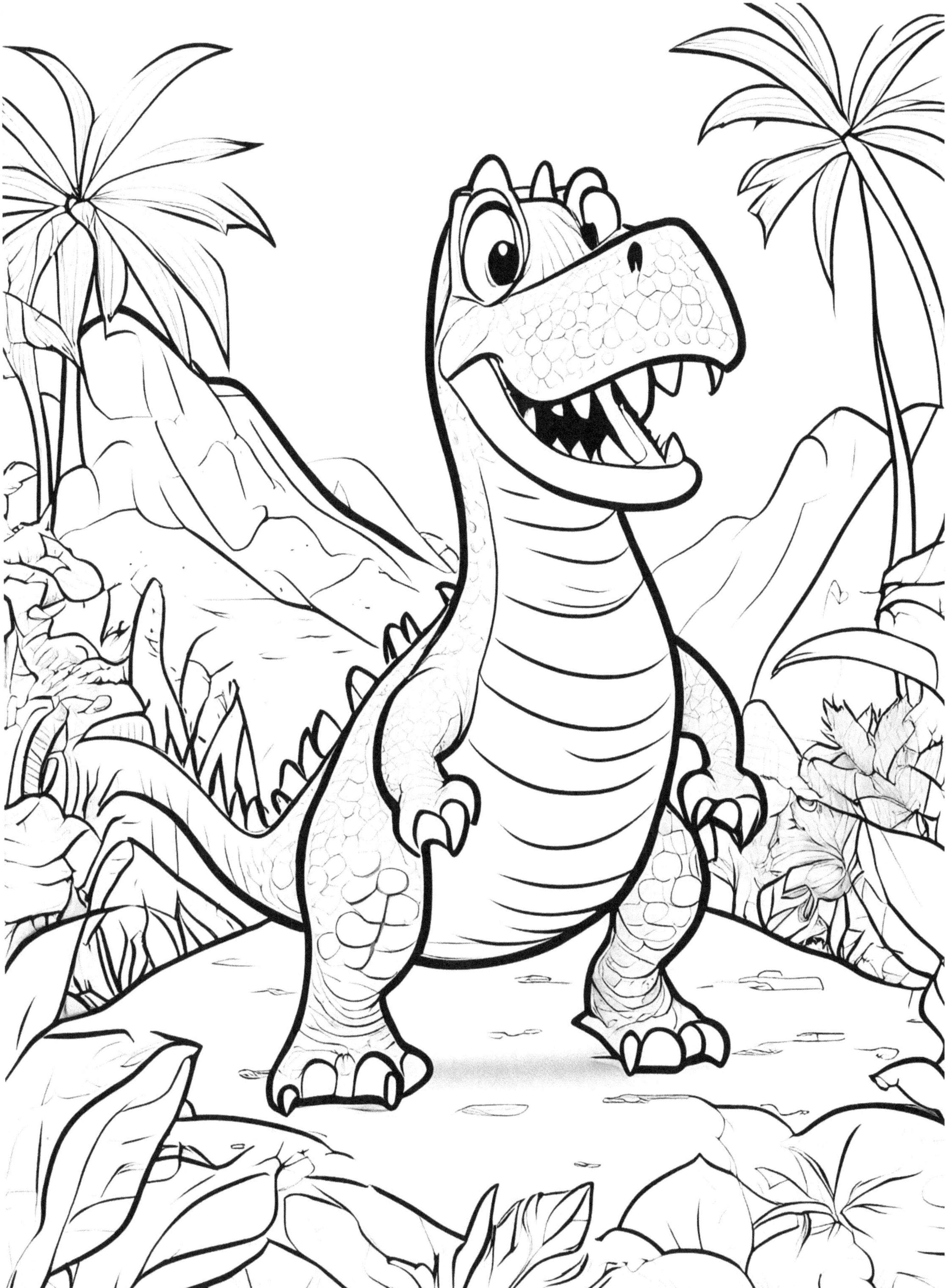

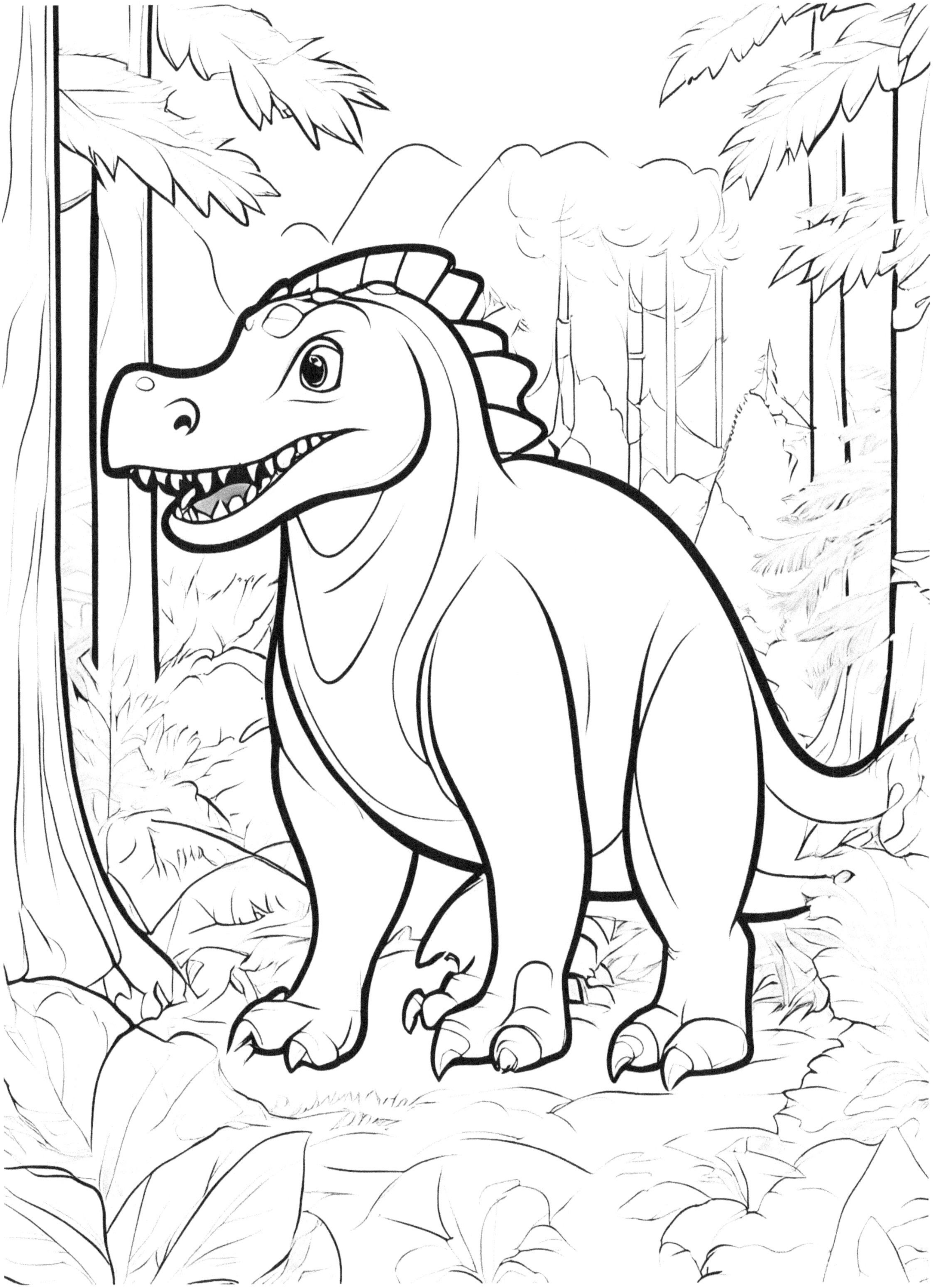

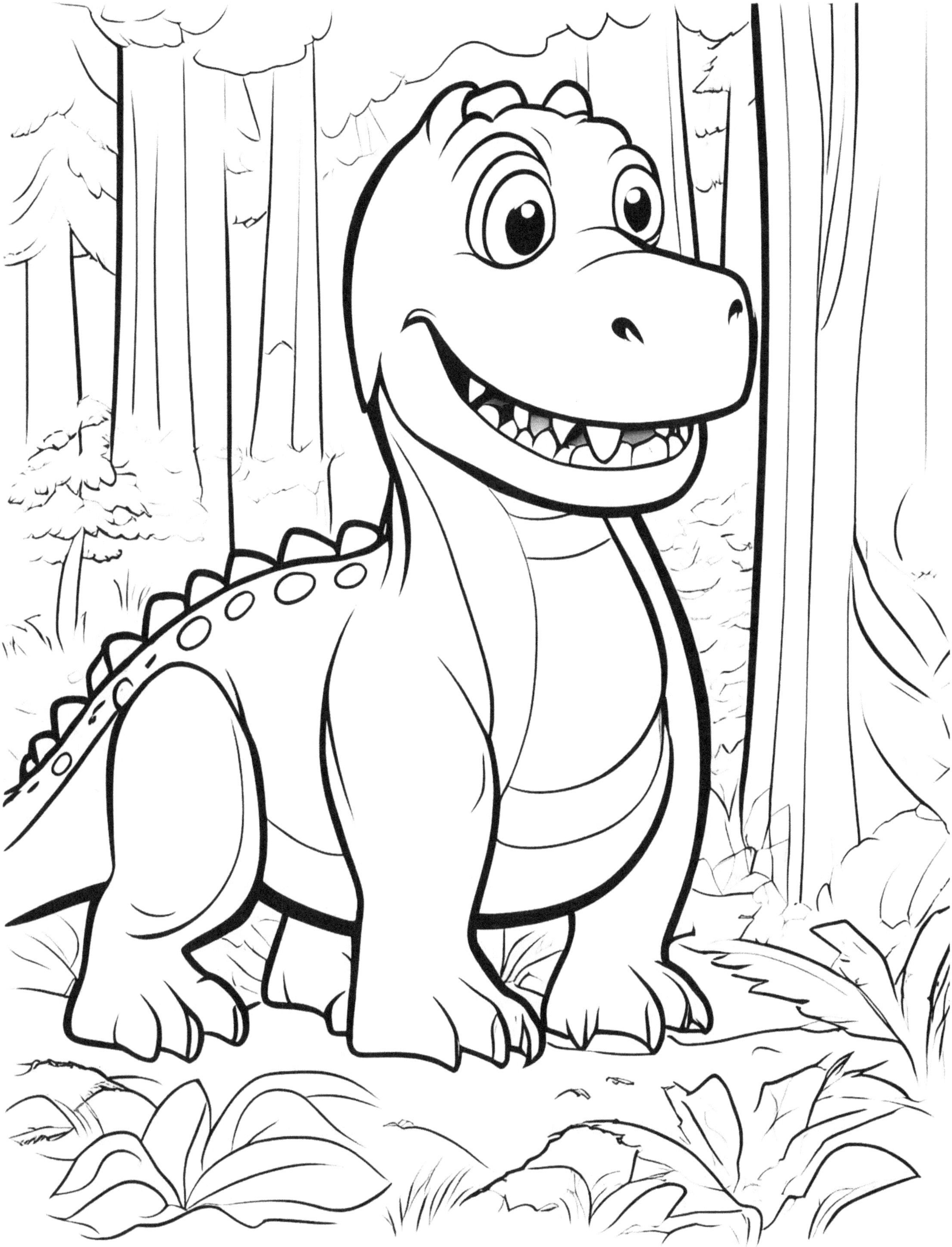

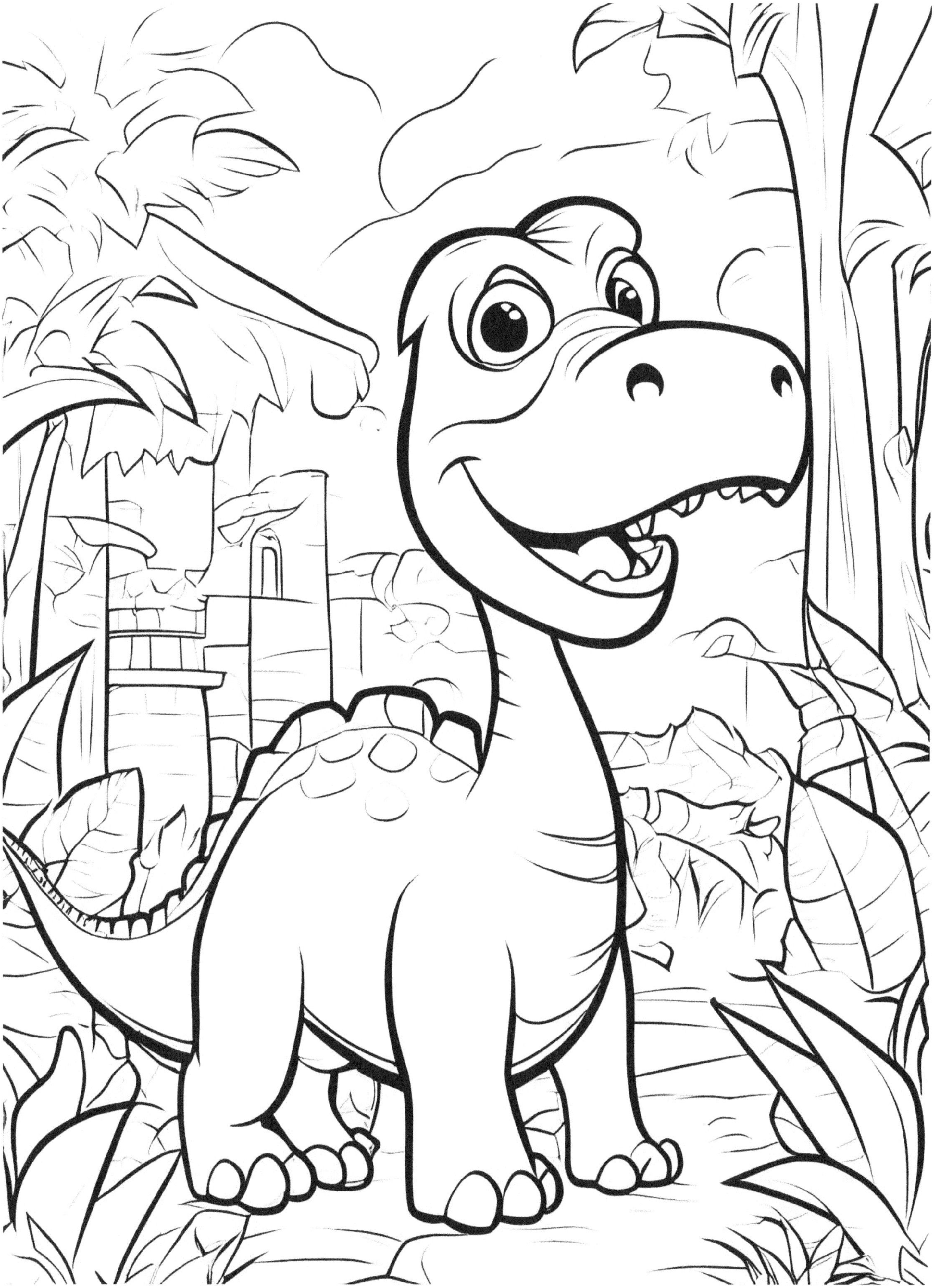

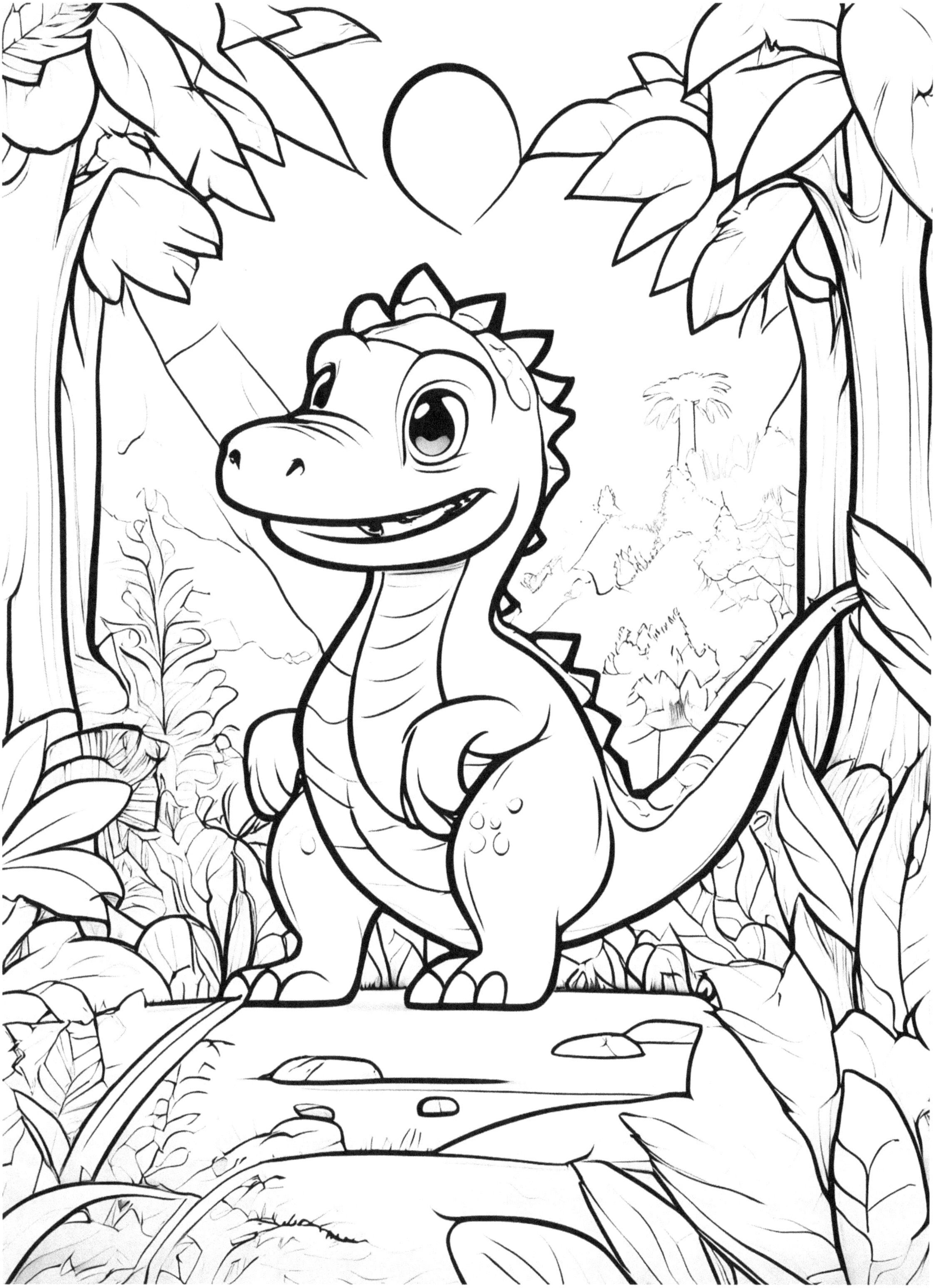

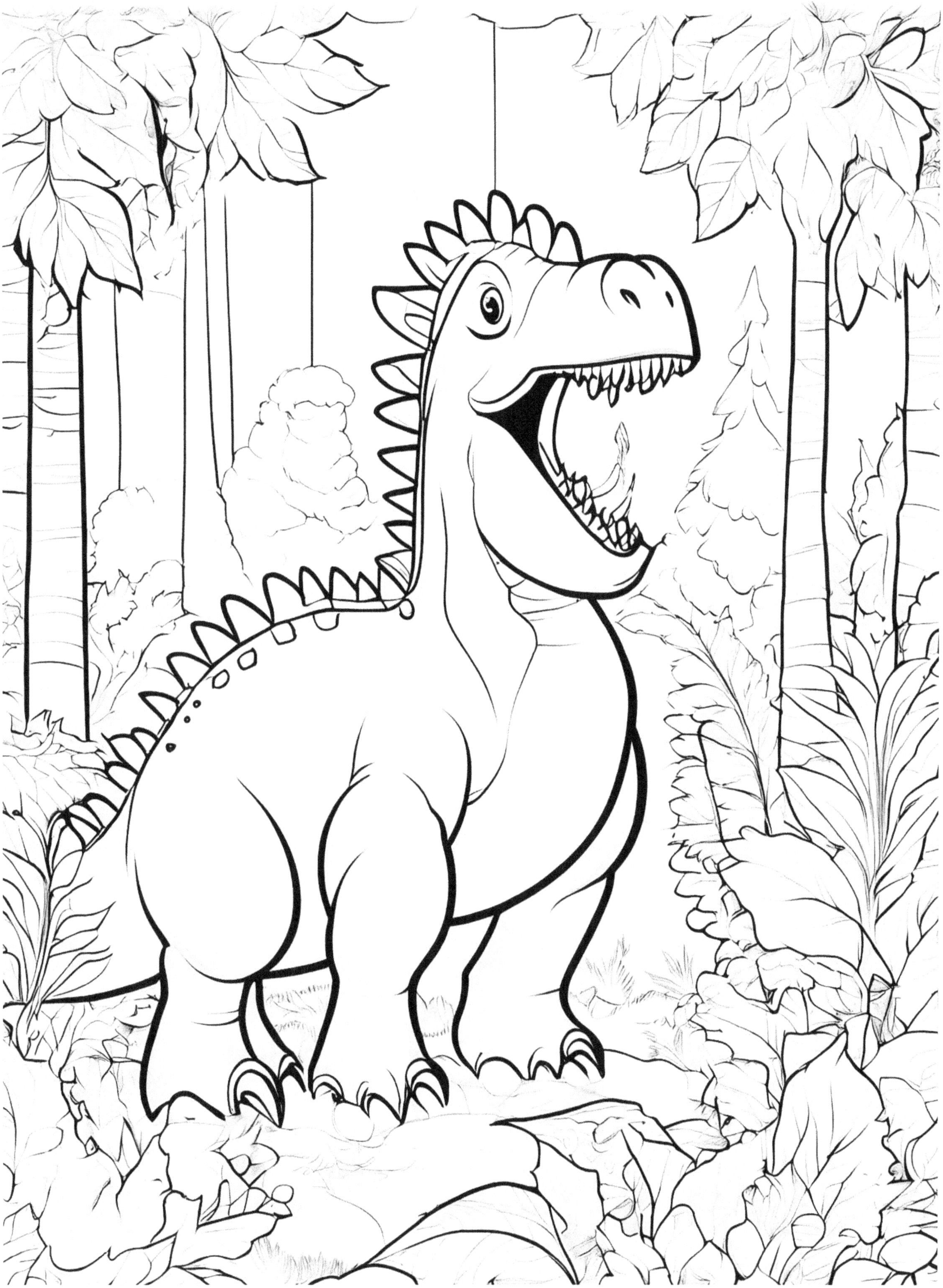

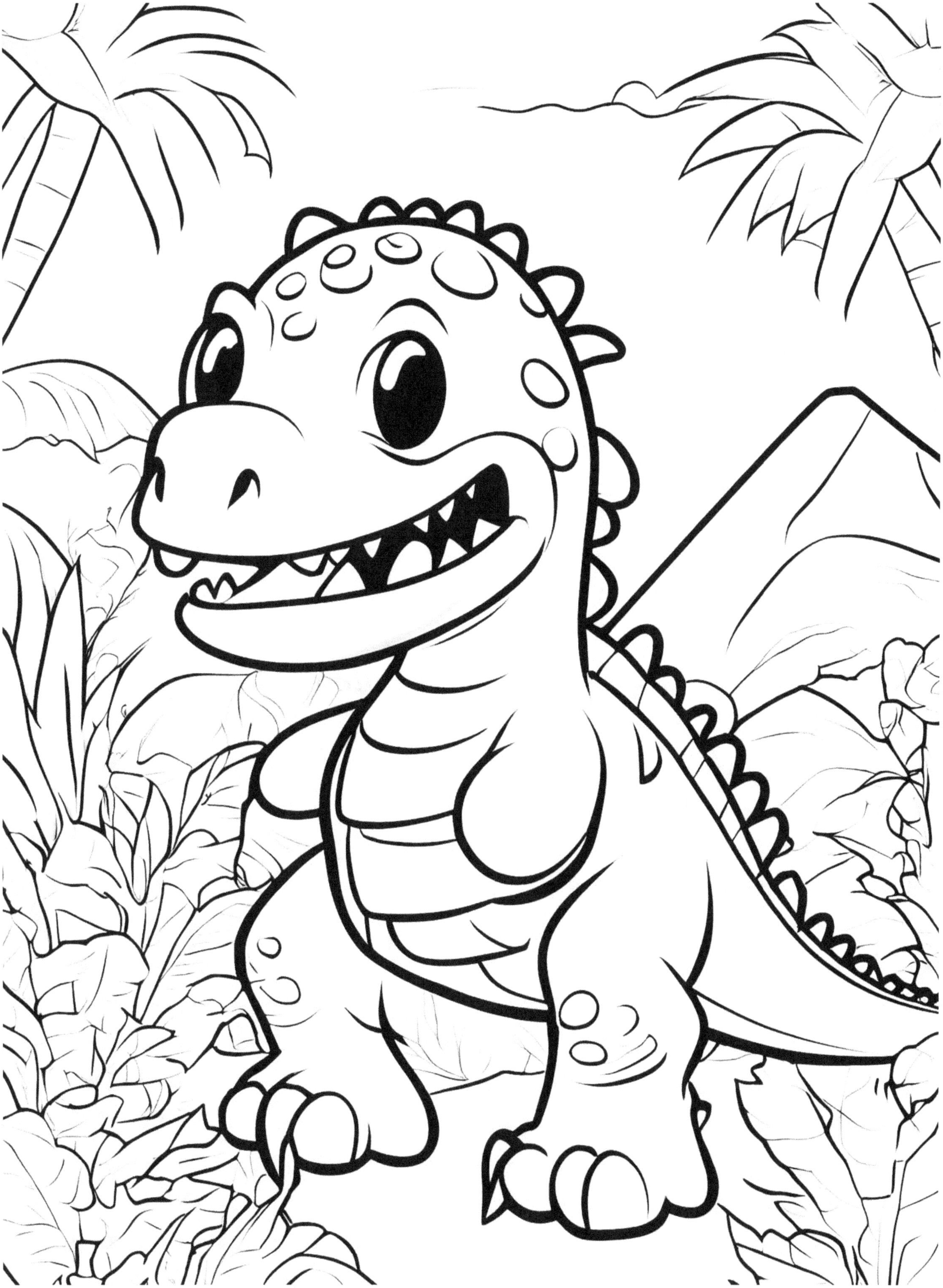

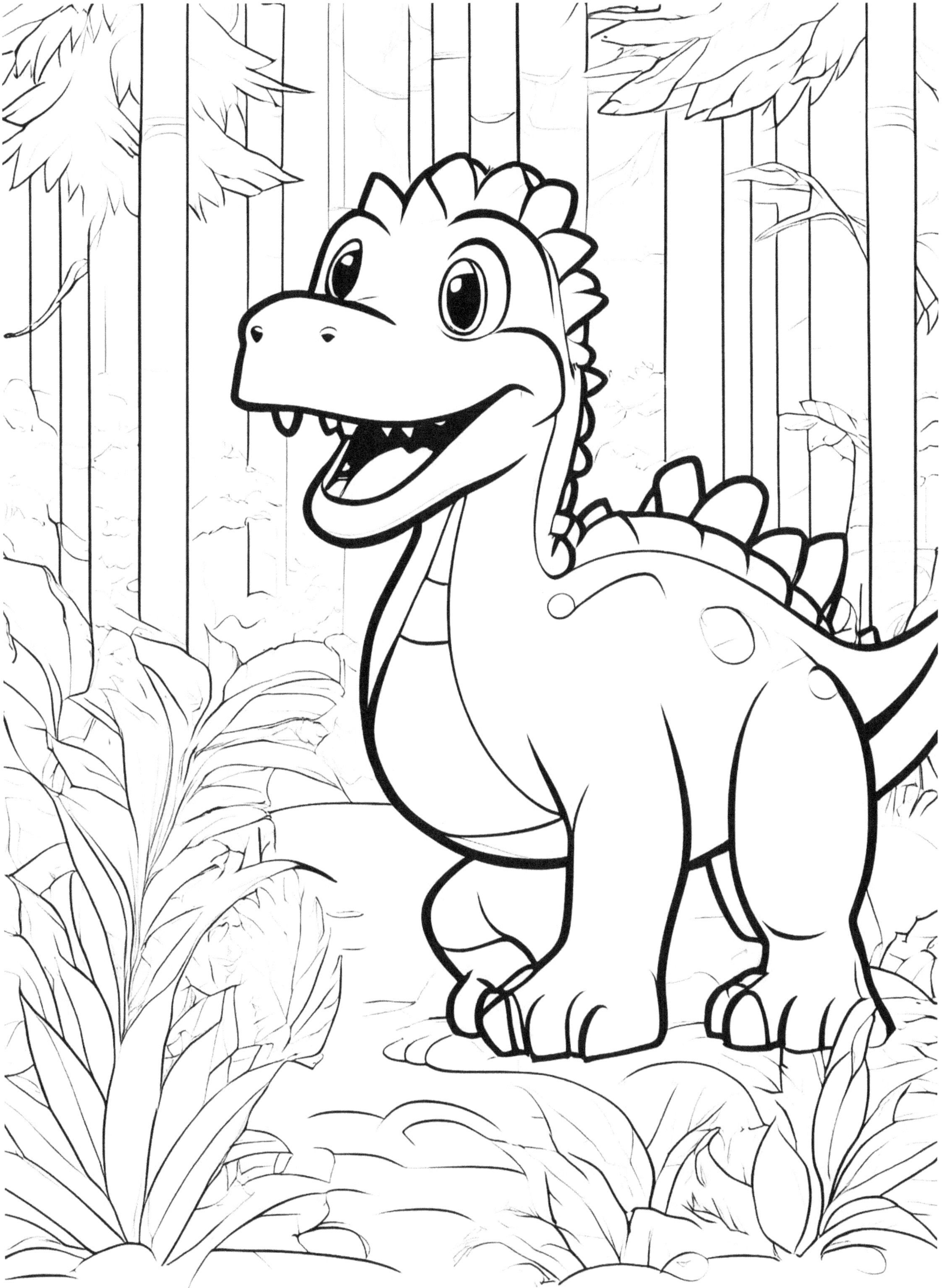

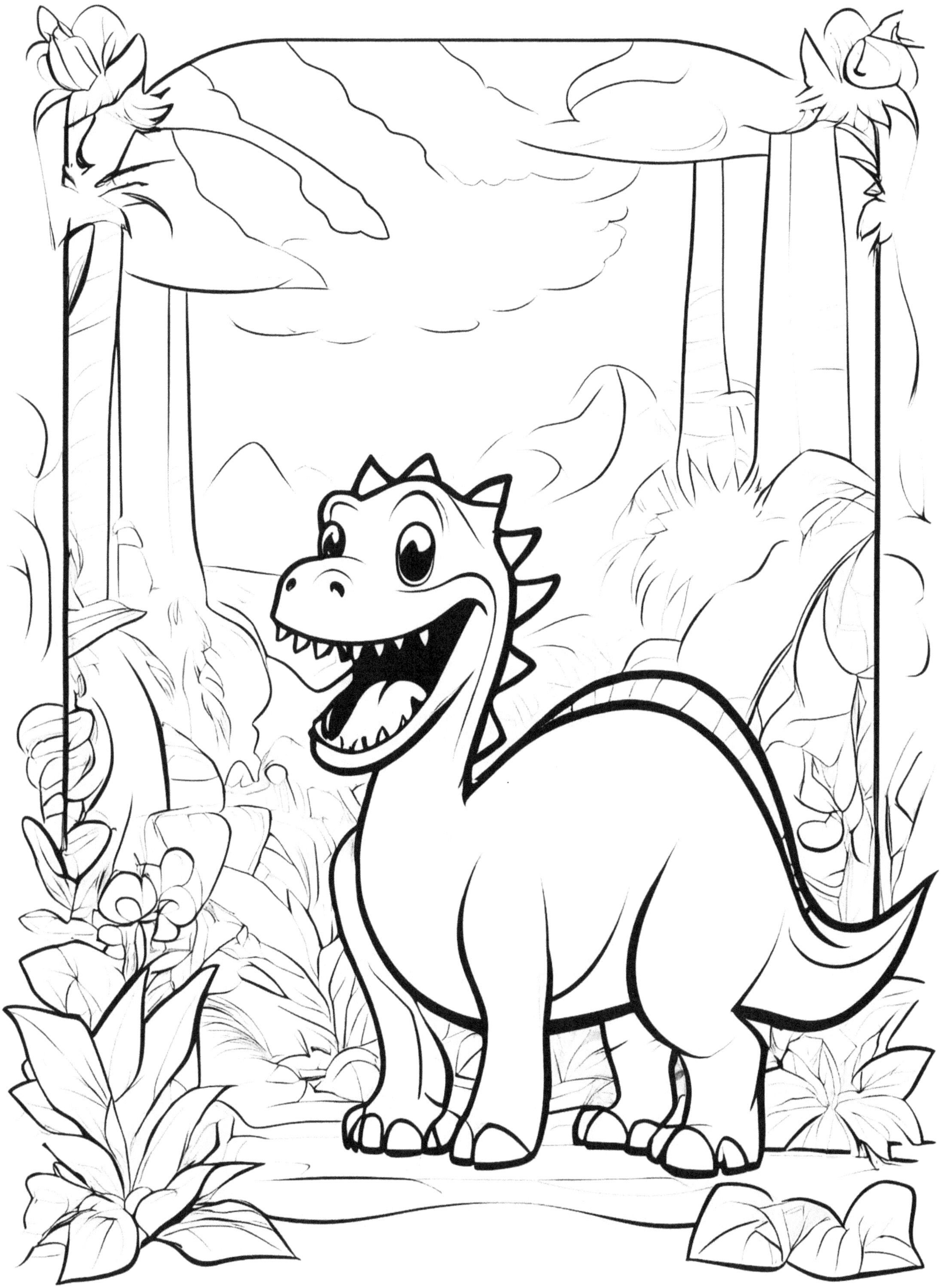

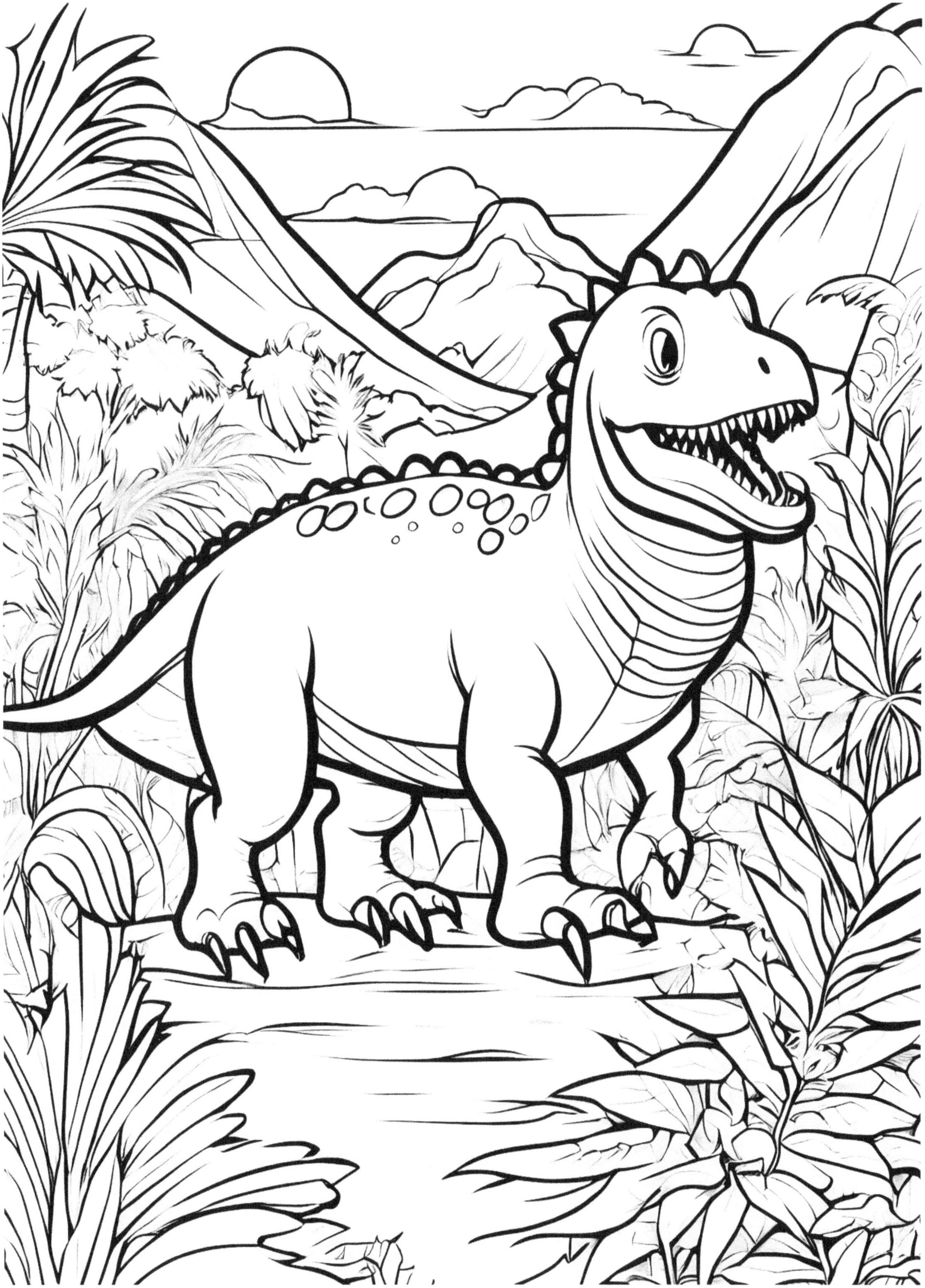

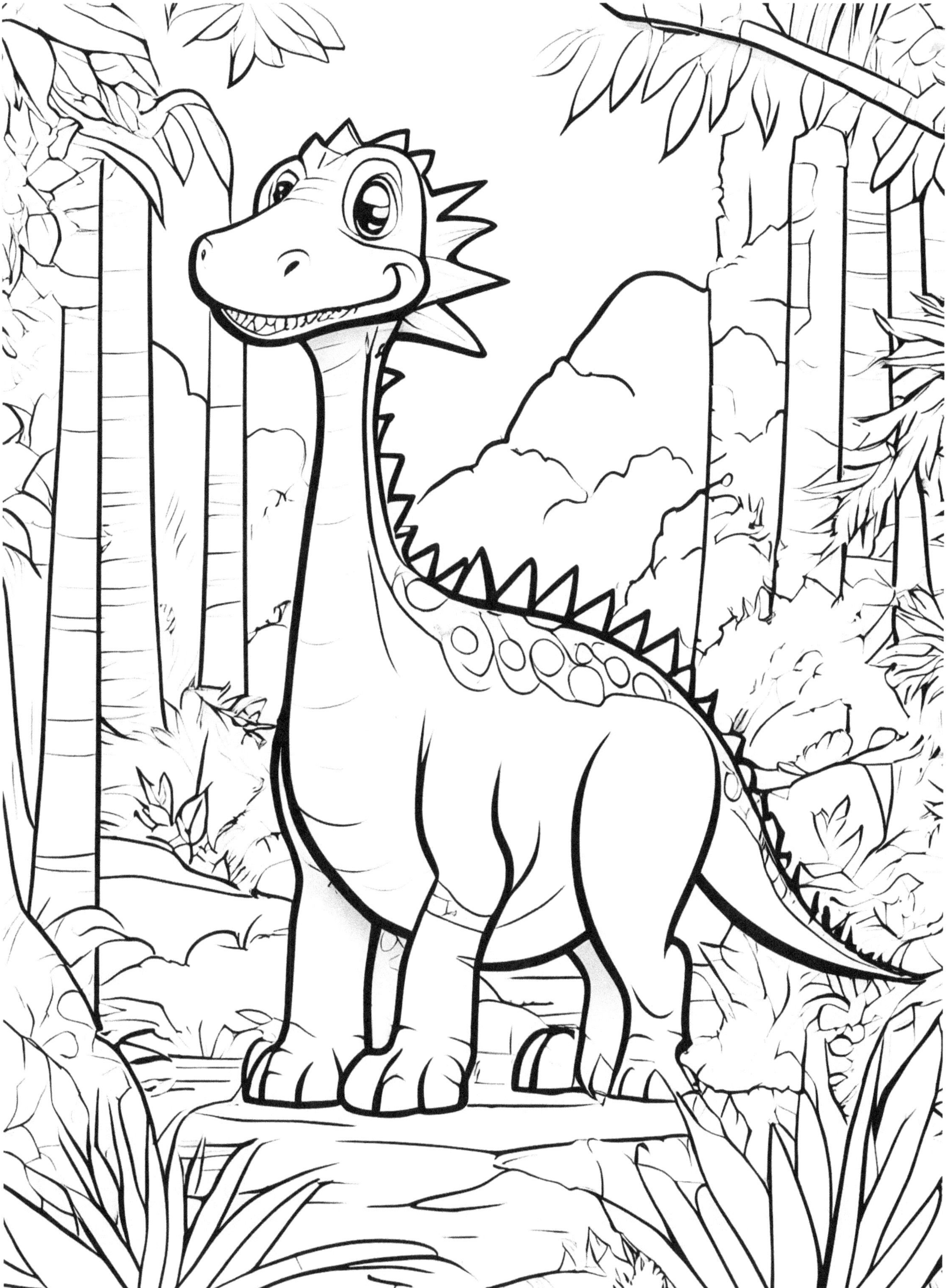

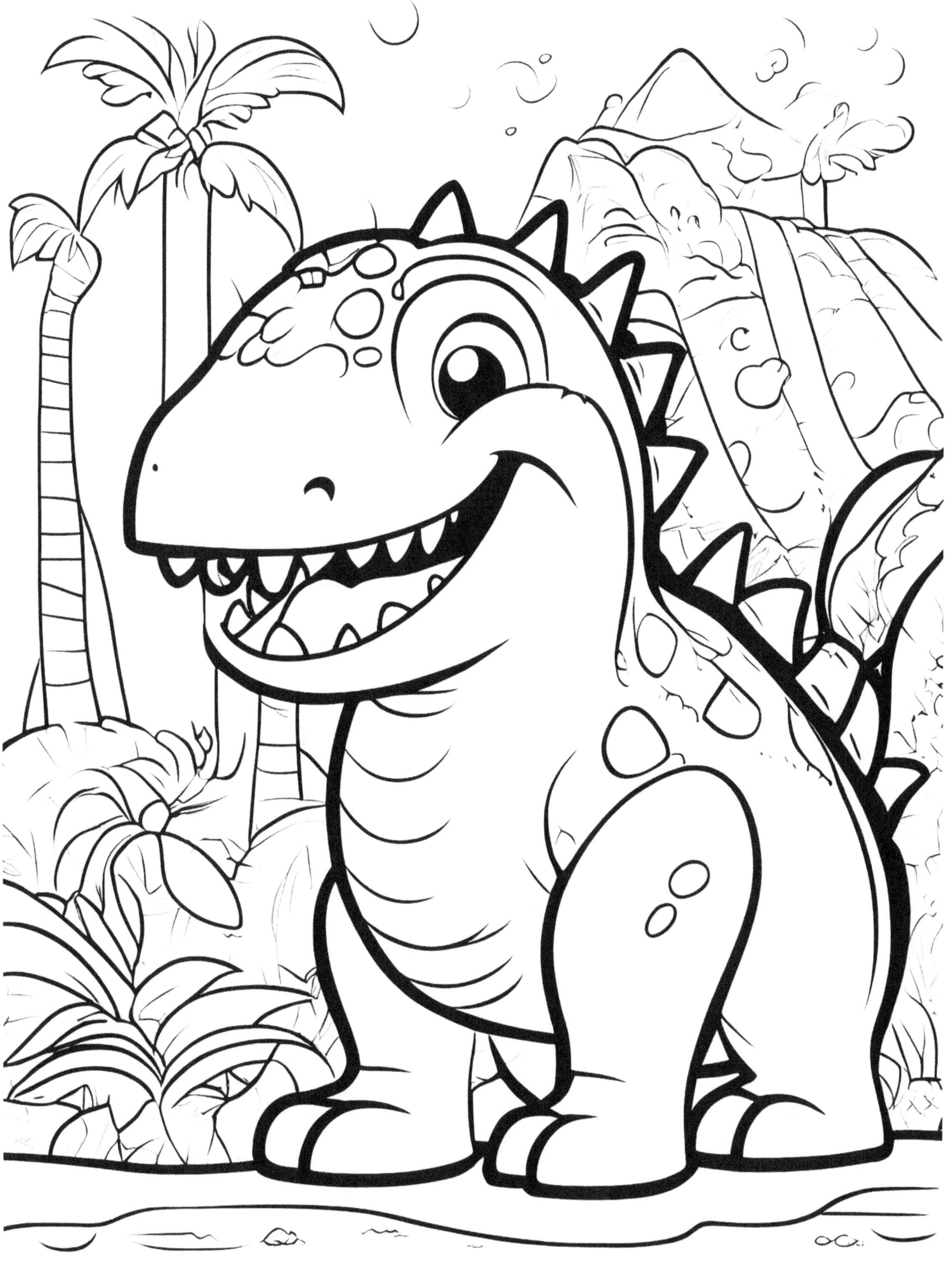

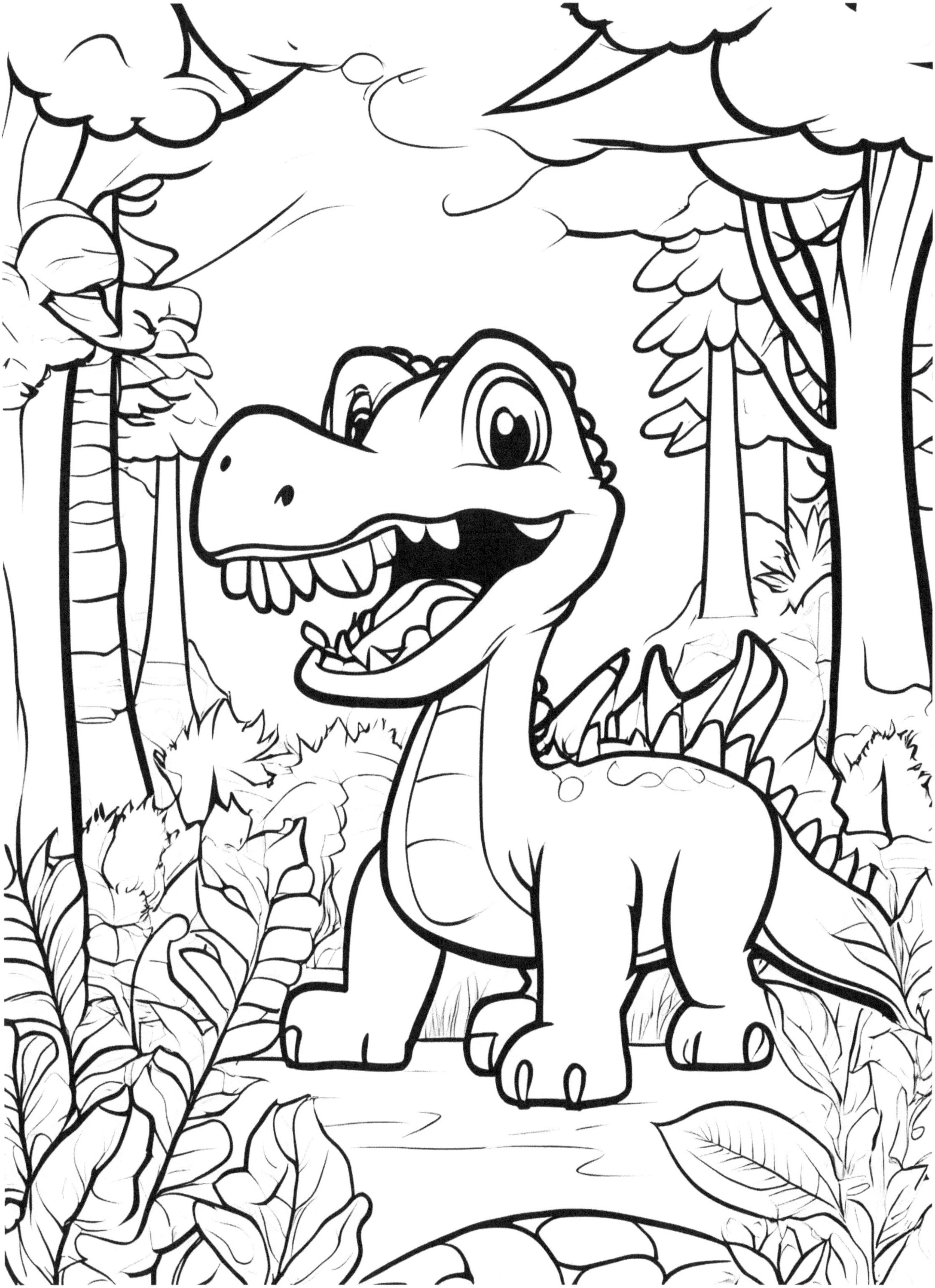

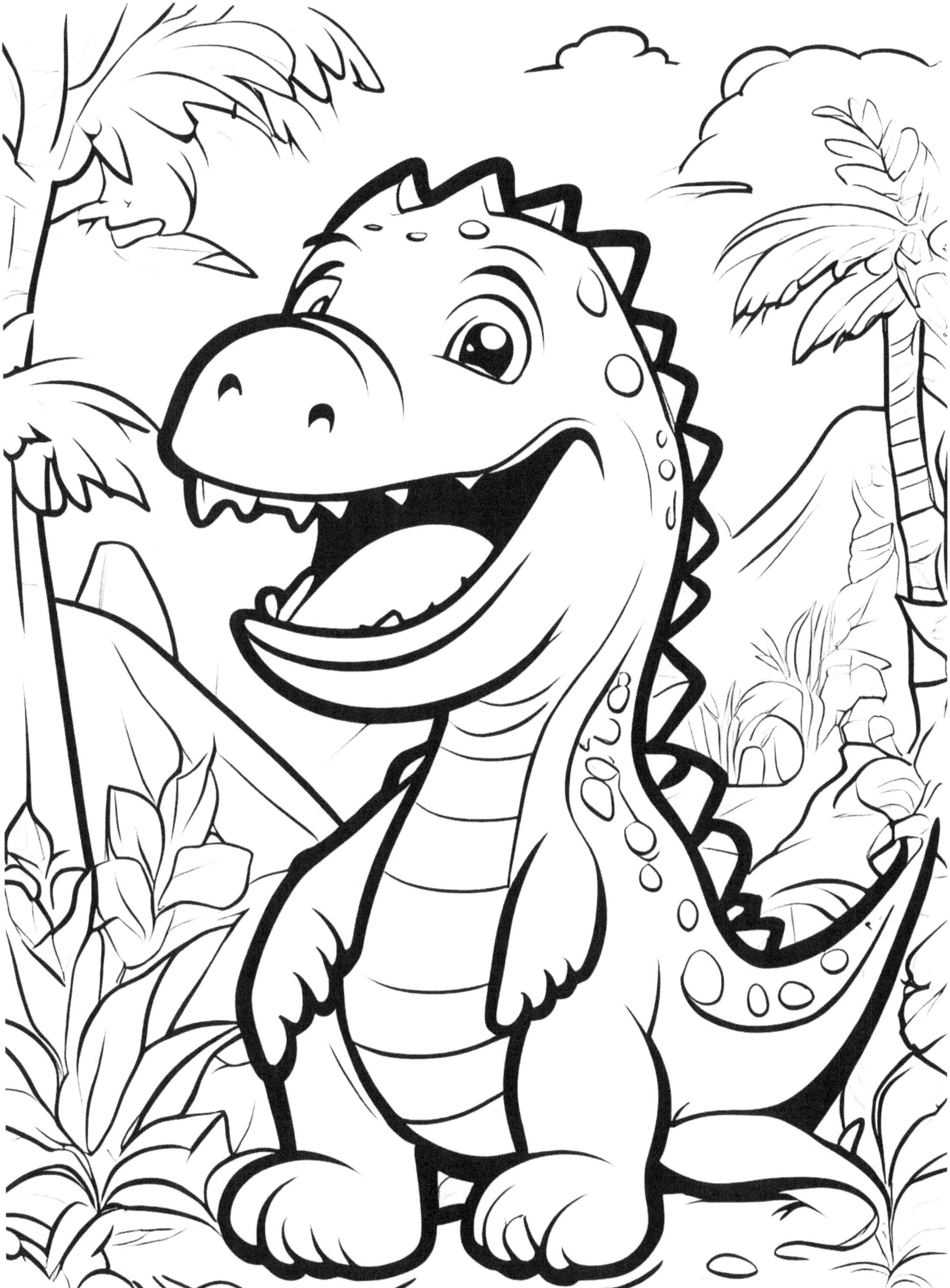

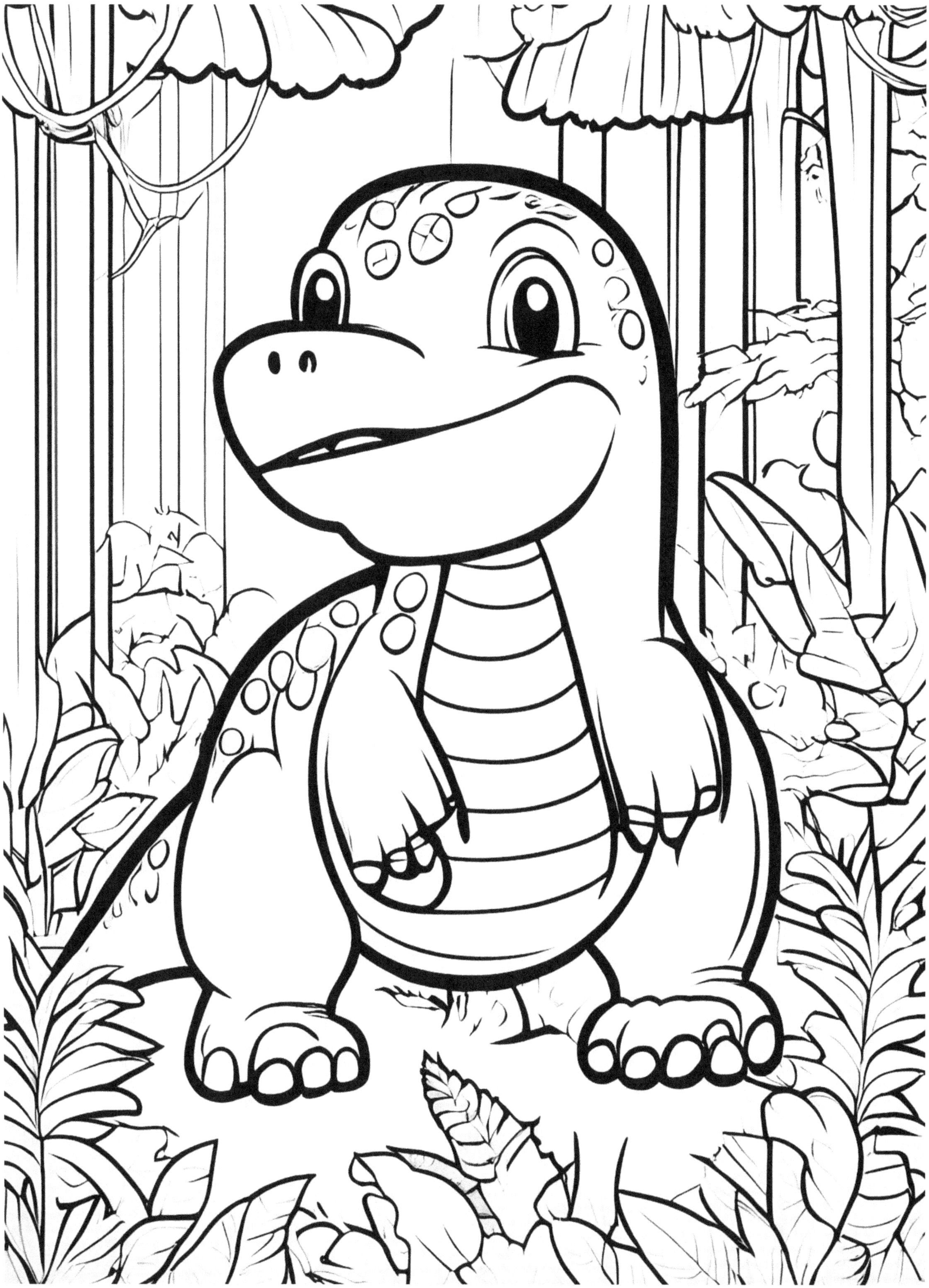

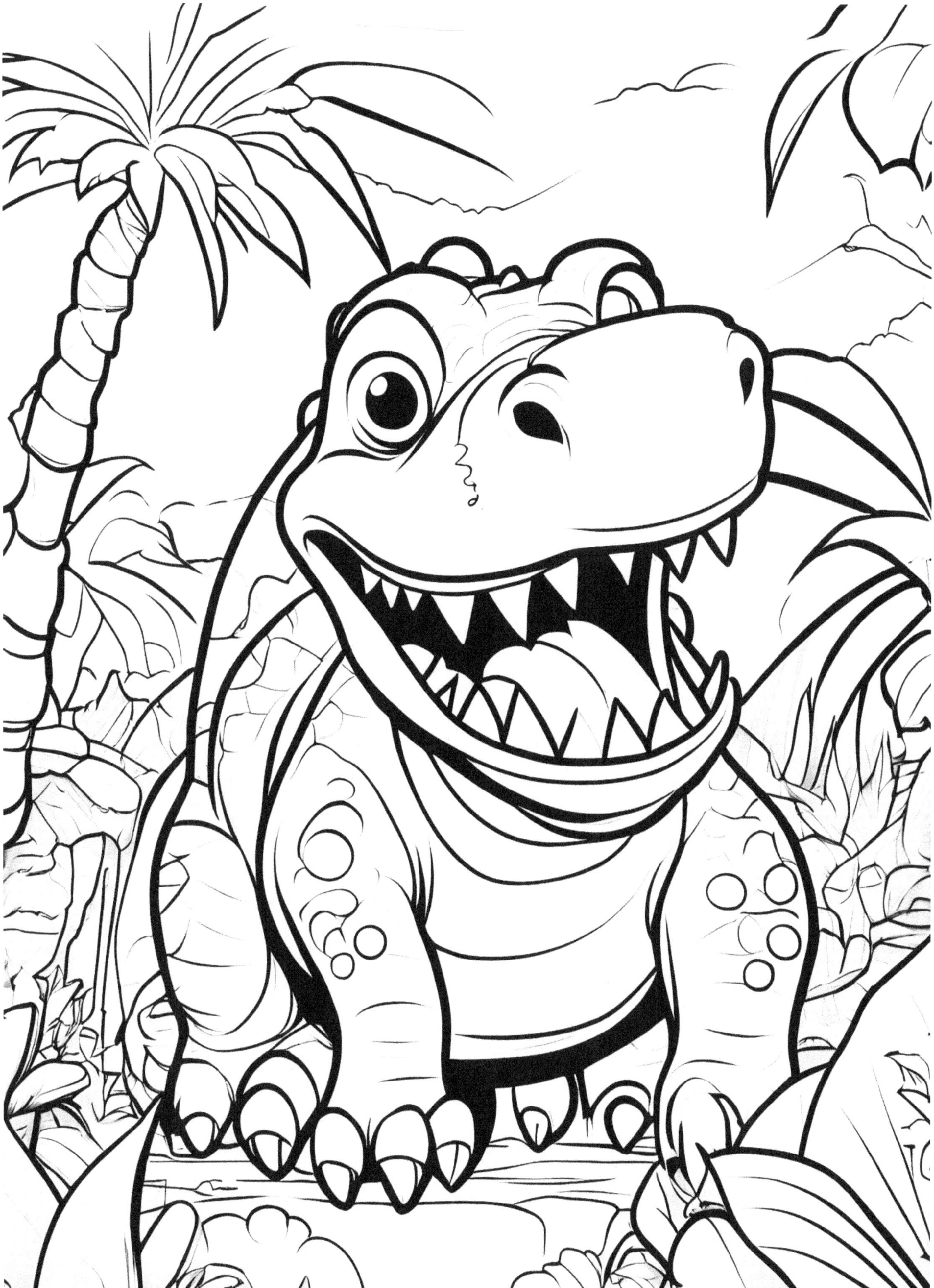

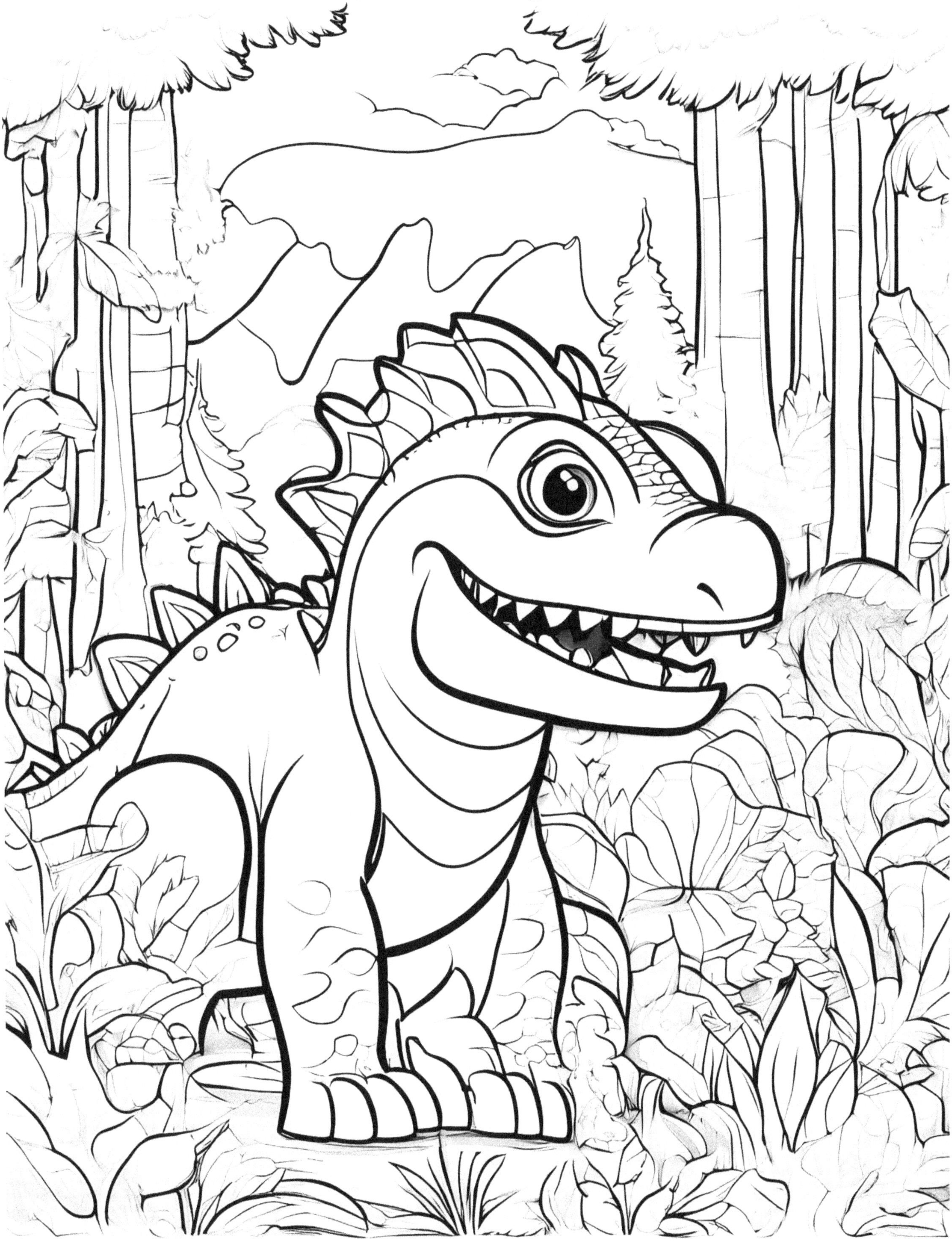

www.ingramcontent.com/pod-product-compliance
Lightning Source LLC
Chambersburg PA
CBHW080956290526
45795CB00009B/2974
9798879762327